五福

five-fold happiness

福祿壽囍財

five-fold happiness

chinese concepts of *luck, prosperity, longevity, happiness,* and *wealth*

by **vivien sung**

chinese translation by **you shan tang**
color photographs by **richard weinstein**

CHRONICLE BOOKS
SAN FRANCISCO

To Mum, Dad, and my dear friend Basquali.
In memory of Tibor.

Library of Congress Cataloging-in-Publication Data available.

ISBN: 0-8118-3526-X

Manufactured in China.

Designed by Vivien Sung.
Calligraphy by You Shan Tang.
Typeset in berthold akzidenz grotesk and sabon.

Distributed in Canada by Raincoast Books
9050 Shaughnessy Street
Vancouver, British Columbia V6P 6E5

10 9 8 7 6 5 4

Chronicle Books LLC
85 Second Street
San Francisco, California 94105

www.chroniclebooks.com

福如東海　壽比南山

May you enjoy good fortune as expansive as the Eastern Sea,
and longevity as long as the Southern Mountain—
fú rú dōng hǎi, shòu bǐ nán shān.

福

luck

祿

prosperity

8 preface 前言
11 introduction 序

250 index 索引
252 acknowledgments 鳴謝
255 biographies 作者簡介

22 luck character「福」字
28 god of luck 福神
32 bat 蝙蝠
36 door gods 門神
42 spring couplet 春聯
45 new year pictures 年畫
46 lucky children 大阿福
48 vase 瓶
50 gourd 葫蘆
52 dragon 龍
54 dragon and lion dances 龍舞 · 獅舞
56 scepter 如意
58 cloud 雲
60 windmill 風車
62 buddha's hand 佛手
64 shrimp 蝦
65 laughing mouth 開口笑
66 fortune cookie 籤語餅
67 oysters 蠔

74 deer 鹿
77 god of prosperity 祿神
80 carp leaping over the dragon's gate 鯉魚跳龍門
82 six「六」字
84 peony 牡丹
86 monkey 猴
88 three ingots 三元
89 rooster 雄雞
90 crab 蟹
91 sticky rice cake 年糕

longevity

104 one hundred long lives
百壽圖

106 god of longevity 壽神

112 pine tree 松樹

116 bamboo 竹

119 plum 梅

120 cypress 柏

122 crane 鶴

125 tortoise 龜

126 peach 桃

130 queen mother of
the west
西王母

132 moon goddess 月神

134 goddess of longevity
女壽神

138 eight immortals 八仙

142 fungus of immortality
靈芝

144 chrysanthemum 菊

146 narcissus 水仙

147 ginseng 人參

148 longevity noodles 長壽麵

150 longevity lock 長命鎖

152 nine「九」字

double happiness

162 double happiness
character
「雙喜」字

167 god of double
happiness
喜神

170 magpie 喜鵲

174 mandarin ducks 鴛鴦

178 phoenix 鳳凰

182 qí lín 麒麟

184 carp 鯉魚

186 spider 蜘蛛

188 firecrackers 爆竹

191 gods of unity and
harmony
和合二仙

194 lotus 蓮

196 date 棗

197 chestnut 栗

198 peanut 花生

199 melons and seeds
瓜類與瓜籽

200 pomegranate 石榴

201 red eggs 紅蛋

204 four-happiness boys
四喜娃

wealth

214 eight「八」字

220 god of wealth 財神

226 coins 古錢

228 money tree 搖錢樹

229 tangerine 橘

232 gold and silver ingots
元寶

233 dumpling 餃子

234 red packet 紅包

238 god liu hai 神仙劉海

242 fish 魚

244 goldfish 金魚

246 fā cái plant 發菜

248 lettuce 生菜

249 beckoning cat 招財貓

前言

從紐約回到澳洲的家時，我買了一件禮物送給我媽媽，一只形狀新奇的時鐘。起

初，她似乎不大敢接受，隨後還用些借口，堅持讓我將禮物轉送其它朋友，她的

反應使我莫名其妙。我甚至有點不悅。經我一再催促，她只簡單地回答說，家裡

不需要另一只時鐘。緊接著她又加上一句，證有些迷信的中國人認為，將鐘作禮

物送人，是觸人霉頭的，因為「鐘」與「終」諧音，送鐘作禮，就造成「為你送

終」的寓意。頓時，我意識到有許多中國的風俗，我根本不懂。

這次失禮的行為，激起我的興趣，去發掘中國文化中各種各樣的象徵形象

，符號以及迷信的傳說。在童年，我所遇到的中國民俗傳統，與我的同齡很不相

同。當我的同伴將他們的牙齒藏在枕頭下，以期待牙齒仙女送錢來時，我則被告

之，把牙齒扔到屋頂上或牀底下。這樣新的牙齒就會或向天，或向地健康地向上

下長。多少年來，在吃晚飯時，我曾呆呆地盯著中國瓷碟，上面描繪著各種

人物、動物和中國字。作為第一代美籍華人，有許多中國的傳統伴隨著我成長

，當時我並不能理解其含意。現在這些事物都成了本書中探討的內容「本書的旨

意，就是想揭示中國文化中這些象徵形象的起源、寓意和傳統的用法。現在我已

經懂得，讓我媽媽自己去選購時鐘了。

preface

When I returned home to Australia after a trip overseas, I brought back a gift for my mother — a rather quirky-looking clock from New York with a Route 66 emblem on it. At first she seemed apprehensive about accepting it, and then on some pretext insisted I give it to another friend. Her response left me puzzled, even slightly offended. When I pressed further, she replied that she simply had no use for another timepiece in the house. And then she added, as though it were an afterthought, that for some superstitious Chinese, sending a clock as a gift is considered an omen of death. As it happens, the word 'clock,' *zhōng*, is phonetically identical to the word 'end,' and combining it with the word 'to send,' *sòng*, creates the phrase 'to send one to one's end.' At that moment it dawned on me that there were many things Chinese I did not understand.

Making this faux pas stimulated my interest in uncovering the rich signs, symbols, and superstitions of Chinese culture. During my childhood I experienced traditions that were peculiarly different from those of my playmates. While my friends hid their teeth under the pillow, expecting money from the tooth fairy, I was told to throw mine on the roof or under the bed, so that the new teeth would grow as they should, up toward the sky or down toward the ground. As a first-generation Chinese Australian, I grew up surrounded by many of the bowls, plates, and other objects that make up the content of this book. All these things inspired me to discover the origins, meanings, and traditional uses of these symbols within Chinese culture; this book is the result. And these days, I leave it to my mother to choose her own clocks.

The characters for luck, *fu*, prosperity, *lu*, and
longevity, *shou*, are integrated into one form.
表現福祿壽的圖案

introduction

Good fortune and auspicious thought are central to all aspects
of Chinese life and culture. The Chinese believe that by layering
their lives with lucky objects and images, they increase their
chances of a happy and prosperous existence. Over the centuries,
a symbolic language has evolved that expresses these ideas
in art, craft, architecture, language, and everyday objects. Lucky
words and phrases were used to create an environment protected
from misfortune, bad omens, and disaster. In the Han dynasty
(206 B.C.– A.D. 220), these feliticious words, phrases, and motifs
began to appear on vessels and utensils, and later spread to
other forms of decorative arts.

      Because the Chinese language consists of many words
distinguished by only a slight variation in tone, it is especially
susceptible to puns and wordplay. Many of the objects and symbols in this book derive their iconic status from puns with lucky
words, depicted visually as rebuses. These pictorial puns, known
as *jí xiáng tú àn*, developed sometime in the Song dynasty (960 –
1279). Typically, they are represented by four Chinese characters
or a combination of objects with little obvious relationship. For
example, a picture of a bat with an ancient Chinese coin represents 'luck before one's eyes,' because the word 'bat' sounds
the same as the word 'luck,' *fú*, and the coin's square center is
known as an 'eye,' *yǎn*.

      The symbols in this book represent the five most sought-
after values in Chinese culture — luck, *fú*, prosperity, *lù*, longevity,
shòu, double happiness, *xǐ*, and wealth, *cái*. The three concepts

fú, lù, shòu are frequently grouped together and represented by their corresponding deities—the God of Luck, the God of Prosperity, and the God of Longevity. These figures are highly revered, and many Chinese throughout the world display their statues or images in their homes. A multitude of rebuses have been created to represent the three values in combination. Their importance is embodied in the saying 'In Heaven there are three lucky stars, on Earth there are *fú, lù, shòu*.'

While the majority of the objects and symbols in this book are traditional, more recently developed icons, such as the number eight and the beckoning cat, which both signify wealth, have also been included. Many of the symbols, old and new, encompass multiple meanings and could appear in several chapters. To simplify matters, I have placed each one in the category that has the strongest resonance with that symbol. In retelling the legends behind the symbols, I have drawn on the best-known ones, as the stories vary from dynasty to dynasty and place to place. All references to New Year are to the Chinese Lunar New Year—a celebration that begins on New Year's Eve and ends on the full moon fifteen days later. In the Western calendar, Chinese Lunar New Year falls on a different date every year, between late January and early March. Dates of dynasty periods are A.D. unless otherwise specified. And finally, the Chinese text is an approximate translation of the English. The standard phonetic system of *pīn yīn* has been used to transcribe all Chinese words into English.

信奉福運和吉兆是中國人整個生活與文化的核心。中國人相信，佩吉祥符物和吉利的形象來營造環境，獲取幸福生活的機會必將大增。千百年來，古兆的象徵和表達手法，一直在不斷演化，廣泛地應用在藝術品、手工藝品、建築、語言以至日用物品等生活的各個方面。

吉祥用語起源於人們對避災禍、化厄運的渴望。這些巧妙的詞語和圖案自漢代就出現在各種器皿用具上，往後則普遍被其它裝飾藝術所採用。

由於中文的許多詞彙，語調變化微妙，正如本書中不少物品、圖案和符號都寓意雙關，所以「雙關語」便層出不窮，寓意雙關的吉祥圖案在宋代得到了大

A rebus representing the God of Luck, the God of Prosperity, and the God of Longevity.

表現福祿壽的圖畫

發展。其典型的手法是由四個中文字構成，而以諧音或以表面無關但卻題而易見的意象聯想來表達。例如由蝙蝠和古錢組成的圖案，就因為「蝠」與「福」諧音、「錢眼」與「眼前」諧音，就用來表達「福在眼前」的寓意。此書將集中介紹以「五福」為主的吉祥象徵符號：福、祿、壽、喜、財。

「五福」中的前三福：福、祿、壽。常被視為最受崇敬的神明—福神、祿神、壽神。人們創造了眾多的內涵，來表現他們。這三尊神的組合壓泛流行，他們的形象普及到世界各地許許多多中國人的家庭裡。俗話說：「天上三吉星，人間福祿壽。」正表明了他們的重要性。

本書中大部份的物件和圖案，均為傳統樣式，也包括了近年出現的象徵「發達」的「八」字和招財貓。不管舊的或新的，許多圖案常集有多種含意於一身，可以分別在本書的不同章節中出現。為子簡化起見，我一般將這些圖案歸類於最能反映其特點的章節之中。鑒於朝朝代代，源遠流長，有關這些吉祥圖案的傳說積累了大量不同的版本，我只能選擇一些最聞名的故事。本書提供中英文對照的雙語解說。漢語拼音方案則作為本書中所有中文詞匯的發音標準。

The three lucky stars: the God of Luck, the God of Prosperity, and the God of Longevity.
三吉星：福祿壽

luck

The character *fú* represents 'good fortune,' 'blessings,' or 'luck.' Since ancient times, the desire for *fú* has been widespread, and its popularity is reflected in many applications of decorative arts, architecture, and clothing. Beginning in the Ming dynasty (1368–1644), a large *fú* character would often be found at entranceways of buildings to bring a continuous flow of good fortune through the door. Phrases and pictures express this thought, such as 'the God of Luck brings fortune,' *fú xīng gāo zhào*, and 'an abundance of luck and long life,' *duō fú duō shòu*. Symbols for luck include the bat, the *rú yì* scepter, the fruit known as Buddha's hand, and the God of Luck.

福，就是福氣、幸運、幸福的意思，被普遍地視作為中華文化的核心意念。自遠古以來，人們就廣泛地流行著「祈福」，這種追求大量地在裝飾藝術、建築和服飾上體現出來。自明朝起，大大的「福」字就已出現在樓房庭園的入口處，目的是讓運氣源源不斷地湧進家門。吉祥的詞句也展現這個理念，例如「福星高照」、「多福多壽」。另外，蝙蝠、如意、佛手和福神，也都被認為是有福氣寓意的圖案。

福到了 = luck has arrived

「福」字 ■ 在中國民俗中，「福」字是非常流行的裝飾。在農曆新年期間，門上、牆上處處都可以看到貼有「福」字。「福」字一般用黑墨寫在棱形紅紙上，並通常被倒著貼，因為「倒」與「到」諧音，所以倒著貼就寓意「福到了」。

(fú dào lè)

luck character / The *fú*, or luck, character is a popular decoration pasted on doors and walls, particularly during New Year. Usually written in black ink on red diamond-shaped paper, it is affixed upside down because the phrase 'to turn upside down,' *dào*, is also a pun on the word 'arrived,' *dào*. An upside-down *fú* therefore signifies 'luck has arrived,' *fú dào lè*.

「福」字的傳說

一次，明太祖朱元璋微服私訪一個小鎮，發現一群人圍著一幅告示大笑不已。仔細一看，原來上面畫了一個捧著西瓜的大腳女人。他受辱氣極，就命令隨從跟蹤這些人到家，並在他們的門外寫上一個「福」字，以便回朝搬兵，將這些人處死。回宮後將此事告訴了馬皇后，但馬皇后心地善良，她傳喚貼身待從和衛士，立即去那個小鎮，在家家戶戶門外都寫上一個「福」字。第二天，皇帝的錦衣衛果然無法判斷誰是嫌犯，只好作罷。於是「福」字救人活命的傳聞馬上傳遍全城。從此，「福」字就成了逢凶化吉的象徵。

此類故事的另一個版本發生在清朝。一個新年的除夕，恭親王府裡的大總管書寫了幾個大大的「福」字，準備貼在王府和庫房的門上。一個家僕一不留神將「福」字貼倒了，恭親王見了大為惱火，傳令立即找出並鞭撻過失者。大總管害怕怪罪到他頭上，便趕緊跪下，急中生智地說，他聽到許多人都誇恭親王壽高福大，這個「福」字倒著貼，乃是吉慶之兆，因為「倒」與「到」諧音，如今「福」真的到（倒）了。恭親王聽完轉怒為喜，不再責罰大總管和家僕們，而代之以每人賞銀五十兩。這天，「福」真的來到了。

legends of the luck character / One day during the Ming dynasty (1368–1644), Emperor Zhu Yuan Zhang was visiting a small town incognito when he noticed a group of people gathered around a poster and laughing uproariously. On closer inspection he saw that they were staring at a caricature of a woman with large feet holding a watermelon. He recognized it at once as his wife. Outraged, he ordered his soldiers to follow the men responsible and write a *fú* character outside the home of each, intending to have his army return the next day to put them to death. He returned to the palace and related the day's events to his wife, Empress Ma. Being a kind-hearted woman, the empress immediately summoned some trusted servants and guards and told them to write the *fú* symbol on the door of every household in the small town. The following day, the emperor's men had no way to identify the culprits. The news quickly spread through the city that the *fú* symbol had saved the men's lives, and it became a talisman for good fortune.

In another version of the legend, one New Year's Eve during the Qing dynasty (1661–1911), the head housemaster of Prince Gong Qin's palace was preparing a few large *fú* characters to be pasted on the palace and storeroom doors. One of the servants accidentally pasted a *fú* character upside down. On seeing this, the prince was enraged and demanded that the offender be found and punished immediately. The housemaster, fearing the blame would ultimately fall on him, quickly offered an explanation. He had heard many people comment on the prince's good fortune, he said. The *fú* character turned upside down was an auspicious omen for his continued luck, because 'upside down,' *dào,* is identical to the word 'arrived.' The prince was delighted, and instead of inflicting punishment he rewarded the housemaster and all the servants with fifty taels of silver each. That day, luck had truly arrived.

福神 ■ 福神和祿神、壽神一起組成三吉星，是最為世人所崇敬的。早期的傳說認為，福神源於木星，而被信奉為給人帶來福運的歲星，所以福神也稱為福星。較晚的傳說則逐漸將福神人格化，至今其形象已衍變成為一身長袍裝束、慈眉悅目、手執大如意或抱著小孩的老人。

god of luck / Along with the God of Prosperity and the God of Longevity, the God of Luck is part of a group of three revered stellar gods. Early legend recounts that the God of Luck, *fú xīng*, originated as a star and was believed to bring good fortune; his name literally means 'lucky star.' In later mythology he took on a human form, and he is now represented as a kind-looking old man wearing a long gown, often holding a *rú yì* scepter or a child.

legends of the god of luck / According to the Yuan dynasty (1279–1368) text *Sān jiào sōu shén dà quán*, 'Collection of Immortals from the Three Beliefs,' the God of Luck is based on a real person, Yang Cheng of Daozhou, Hunan Province, in the Western Han dynasty (206 B.C.–A.D. 8). An imperial edict declared that dwarfs be sent to the Emperor Wu Di's palace to serve as slaves and entertain the royal family. This caused the dwarfs' parents much grief and hardship. When Yang Cheng assumed office as governor of the prefecture, he petitioned the emperor, stating that short people were the emperor's subjects, not his slaves. The emperor was deeply moved and subsequently dispensed with slavery. People were extremely grateful to Yang Cheng for reuniting their families and deified him as the God of Luck. The worship of his image spread to other regions of the country over the dynasties. Depending on the source, the story varies slightly as to the dynasty or the Chinese characters for Yang Cheng's name. Later, in the Tang dynasty (618–907), the famous poet Bai Ju Yi wrote a poem in his honor titled 'The People of Daozhou,' *Dào zhōu mín*.

⟨⟨⟨⟩⟩⟩

In another origin of the story, the God of Luck is one of the 'Three Officials', *sān guān*, popularized by Zhang Dao Ling, the founder of Taoism in the Eastern Han dynasty (25–220). The three Taoist gods are the 'Heavenly Official who grants fortune,' 'the Earthly Official who pardons wrongdoing,' and the 'Water Official who dispels danger.' The 'Heavenly Official who grants fortune,' *tiān guān cì fú,* was most enthusiastically welcomed by the masses and later came to be known as the God of Luck.

福神的傳說

根據元代的《三教源流搜神大全》記載，福神源於西漢的真實人物，湖南道州刺史楊成。當時，漢武帝曾下詔，要道州每年進貢侏儒數百人入宮，作為皇家的宮奴玩戲。這對侏儒，尤其貧窮的雙親極為悲慘。楊成擔任刺史之後，即以表奏聞漢武帝說：「臣按《五典》，本土只有矮民，無矮奴也。」漢武帝深受感悟，隨即廢了貢侏儒之詔。百姓十分感激楊成使他們家庭團聚，把他奉為福神，為他繪像供養。從此，這種風俗流行到其它地區，超越了漢朝。之後的唐朝著名詩人白居易甚至撰詩歌詠《道州民》。至於「楊成」還是「陽城」，西漢還是中唐，各種史料出處不同，描述的故事也略有出入。

另一傳說起源於道教所信奉的「三官」，這三位尊神包括天官賜福、地官赦罪和水官解厄。東漢道教的創始人張道陵將「三官」的信仰大力推廣，一直流傳至今，其中尤以「天官賜福」最受百姓歡迎，於是就演變成著名的福神。

蝙蝠 bat *(biān fú)* = 福 luck *(fú)*

蝙蝠 ■ 在中國，蝙蝠是個象徵福氣的符號，因為「蝠」與「福」諧音。兩隻蝙蝠相對的圖案象徵「雙福」。紅蝙蝠更被視為吉兆，因為人們相信紅色能驅魔祛邪，而且「紅」與「洪」諧音。成雙的蝙蝠與古錢放在一起，寓意「福在眼前」，因為中國古錢中間的方孔叫「眼」，而「錢」與「前」諧音。十六世紀完成的古代醫書《本草綱目》曾記載：蝙蝠能存活相當久，而牠的血液、膽囊和翼翅均具有藥效，能明目和延壽，所以蝙蝠又與長壽密切關聯。

bat / The bat is a symbol of good fortune because the word 'bat,' *biān fú,* is a play on the word 'luck,' *fú.* A drawing of two bats facing each other represents 'double luck,' *shuāng fú.* A red bat is an especially lucky omen because red is believed to be the color that wards off evil and 'red' is pronounced the same as 'vast,' *hóng.* Together, a bat paired with a coin means 'luck before your eyes,' *fú zài yǎn qián.* The bat is also associated with longevity because the 'Book of Herbal Medicine,' *Běn cǎo gāng mù,* written at the end of the sixteenth century, states that the bat lives to a great age and its blood, gall bladder, and wings have medicinal benefits for eyesight and long life.

bat / Five bats grouped together create the extremely auspicious and popular motif 'five good fortunes,' *wǔ fú* — longevity, wealth, health, love of virtue, and natural death. The phrase 'may the five fortunes arrive at one's door,' *wǔ fú lín mén*, is a common wish. When the five bats are arranged in a circle around the Chinese character for longevity, the result is a rebus for *wǔ fú pěng shòu*, an extremely powerful motif for good fortune and longevity. An image of five bats flying above a round box or container signifies 'harmony and the five fortunes,' *wǔ fú hé hé*, because 'box' and 'harmony' both sound the same, *hé*.

蝙蝠 ■ 五只蝙蝠圍成一圈，則構成廣為流行的吉祥圖案《五福臨門》——長壽、富裕、健康、美德和善終。當五只蝙蝠圍著「壽」字排列，就創造出一「五福捧壽」的寓意，成為「福」與「壽」的精彩設計。五只蝙蝠盤旋在圓盒之上，寓意「五福和合（盒）」，因為「盒」與「合」諧音。

五福捧壽

= five fortunes surround longevity (*wŭ fú pĕng shòu*)

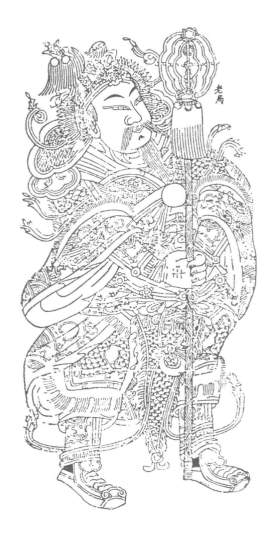

door gods / Images of door gods protect people's homes against evil spirits and general misfortune. Originating in the Eastern Han dynasty (25–220), they were engraved on peach-wood and hung on doors. Beginning in the Song dynasty (960–1279), their portraits were drawn in ink on red paper, and later they were machine printed. They are usually put up at New Year.

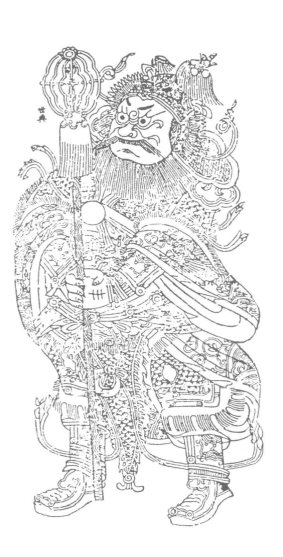

門神 ■ 在農曆新年，人們總要去買一對門神像貼在門口，以祛邪、保家、避厄運。門神像起源於東漢，人們將門神雕刻在桃木板上，掛於門前。從宋代開始，門神像即用墨直接畫在紅紙上。現代的門神像皆用機器印刷。

門神的傳說

傳說唐太宗晚上常聽到寢宮門外有鬼魅號呼，為此整夜無法安睡，且心有餘悸。群臣均為皇帝的健康和安全格外擔憂。兩位武將，秦瓊和尉遲恭（也有說是秦叔寶和尉遲敬德）毫不畏懼，出班奏請，願戎裝立於宮門外，整夜把守警衛。唐太宗終於睡了幾夜的好覺，並嘉獎了這二位大將。為了免除他們徹夜無眠的辛勞，唐太宗傳詔畫工，畫出兩人全副盔甲、手持武器的全身像，貼於宮門外，從此宮內夜夜平安無事，邪祟以息。而這兩位忠誠守衛者也被奉為門神的象徵。不久家家戶戶也都掛上了他們倆的肖像。

legend of the door gods / Emperor Tai Zong of the Tang dynasty (618–907) was disturbed one night by restless demons lurking outside his bedroom. The ministers of state were extremely concerned for the emperor's health and safety. Two guards who were not afraid of ghosts, Qin Qiong and Yu Chi Gong (known in some areas as Qin Shu Bao and Yu Chi Jingde), stepped forward and declared they would stay up all night and keep watch. After several undisturbed nights, the emperor commended the two brave men. Believing he should no longer impose sleepless nights on them, he ordered a painter to draw portraits of the guards equipped with their weapons and clad in full armor. The paintings were pasted on the palace gates, and no further commotion was heard from the spirits. These two loyal subjects were venerated as door gods, and soon many homes displayed their images.

legends of the door gods / According to 'The Classic of Mountains and Sea,' *Shān hǎi jīng,* on Dusu Mountain there was an enormous peach tree whose branches formed an archway through which evil spirits passed back and forth between the spirit world and earth. Fearing the evil spirits would harm people on earth, the Heavenly Emperor assigned the brothers Shen Tu and Yu Lei to guard the passage. If the spirits created any disturbances, the two would bind them with rope and feed them to the tigers at the bottom of the mountain. Later, because of the brothers' bravery, Shen Tu and Yu Lei's portraits were engraved onto peachwood and hung on doors for protection and peace. Yu Lei is traditionally on the left and Shen Tu on the right.

In another variant of the story, the giant peach tree on Dusu Mountain yielded large and sweet peaches that bestowed immortality. On the northeast side of the mountain lived a cruel bandit named Ye Wang Zi, who terrified the people and claimed to be the king of the mountain. One day he heard of the magic peaches and ordered his men to retrieve some of the treasures. They were challenged by the brothers Shen Tu and Yu Lei, who laughed in their faces and drove them away. Ye Wang Zi was furious. He immediately sent three hundred men to do battle with the brothers, who once again defeated the attackers. Craving revenge, Ye Wang Zi dispatched his men dressed as terrifying demons on a dark and gusty night. The brothers heard a rustling noise outside and were startled to see an ominous throng of ghosts with green eyes and red hair. They wasted no time and swiftly tied up the 'ghosts' and fed them to the tigers below. News of the brothers' heroic efforts spread, and later their images were inscribed on peachwood charms to protect humans and scare away evil spirits.

門神的傳說

據《山海經》記載：東海度朔山上有一棵碩大無比的桃樹，樹幹蟠曲，茂葉覆蓋，綿廷三千里，拱型的枝幹彎向東北，形成一座「鬼門」，山上萬鬼均經由此門出入。天帝怕鬼魅擾亂人間，就派神荼、郁壘倆兄弟把守此門。遇到無端造惡、殘害人類的惡鬼，兄弟倆就用葦索把它們綁起來，送往山下去餵虎。後來，兄弟倆的英雄形象被人們雕刻在桃木板上，懸掛於門前，以求御兇魅、保平安。傳統上，郁壘在左，神荼在右。

有關度朔山神荼、郁壘的傳說還有另一個版本：兄弟倆精心培育的大桃樹最終結出了又甜又大的仙桃，吃後能長生不死。度朔山的東北面，住著一個殘忍而令人恐懼的野王子。一天，他聽說吃了桃子能成仙，馬上命令他的手下去奪取這些寶物。然而他們遭遇到兄弟倆強有力的反擊，兄弟倆一面大笑，一面將他們撞下山去。野王子氣極欲狂，立即又派三百人馬去挑戰兄弟倆，但是再戰再敗。野王子復仇心急，密令手下人馬裝扮成面目猙獰的鬼怪，等到半夜月黑風急時，上山襲擊。兄弟倆聽到門外有颯颯的謀音，開門一看，一大群綠眼黑髮的惡鬼撲面而來。兄弟倆不畏懼使命，毫不畏懼地抓住這些惡鬼，敏捷地捆起來送去餵虎。後來，兄弟倆的英雄事跡傳開了，他們的形象被雕刻在桃木板上，掛立於門的兩邊，以示驅災壓邪保平安之意。

春聯 ■ 春聯亦名「門對」、「春帖」，是一種在農曆新年除夕，掛於門口兩邊的詩詞聯句。典型的春聯一般由四字、五字或七字組成一聯（特別場合下可以多到五百字一聯），一律寫在紅紙上（因為紅色代表吉祥）以祈求福運連年，財源廣進，生意興隆。貼在門框上方的橫批通常為四字。春聯的對子必須在字數、句法、組合和結構上對仗工整。其內容可以包括任何祈望，從喜慶、長壽、富足、豐收以至多子多孫。

spring couplet / *Chūn lián*, spring couplets, are poems hung in pairs, one on each side of an entryway, on New Year's Eve. Typically four, five, or seven characters in length, though occasionally as long as five hundred, they attract wealth, good fortune, and abundance to households or businesses. A third horizontal strip with four characters that distill the essence of the couplet is mounted above the doorway. The pair must be identical in character count, composition, syntax, and structure, and are usually on red paper, since red is a propitious color. The couplets may express any wish, such as the desire for happiness, longevity, wealth, good harvests, or an abundance of children.

This spring couplet reads, 'The God of Luck protects the good fortune of the entire family. Wishing wealth and happiness to all families.'

一副春聯：「福星高照全家福，恭禧發財萬戶歡」

春聯 ■ 春聯從桃符演化而來。相傳最早的一副春聯產生在五代，後蜀主孟昶命翰林學士辛寅匯題寫桃符板時，覺得所寫的詞句欠佳，便親自提筆，重新寫了一副更為喜慶的聯語：「新年納餘慶，嘉節號長春」。從此以後，人們就沿襲成風。到了明代春聯則大為流行。明太祖甚至在新年除夕出外微服私訪，觀聯盡興。

spring couplet / Spring couplets evolved from traditional peachwood door god charms, *táo fú*. In the Song dynasty (960–1279), red paper replaced the peachwood plaques. In the Five Dynasties period (907–960), the first spring couplet was conceived by Lord Meng Chang of the state of Later Shu, who ordered an official to write a couplet on a peachwood plaque. Meng Chang was dissatisfied with the couplet and took it upon himself to pen a more pleasing verse. From that time onward, people followed his example, and by the Ming dynasty (1368–1644), the custom of inventing one's own spring couplets had become commonplace. Emperor Tai Zu of the Ming dynasty was even said to venture out incognito on New Year's Eve to appreciate the spring couplets displayed on doorways.

new year pictures /

Depicting scenes of fortune and prosperity, New Year pictures, *nián huà*, were typically wood-cut prints, though they are now machine printed. Originally door god charms carved in peach-wood, their subjects broad-ened, and by the Song dynasty (960–1279) depicted a variety of themes from daily life and society, including good harvests, birds and flowers, landscapes, and fairy tales, as well as wishes for good fortune, longevity, and marital bliss. The cities of Taohuawu in Jiangsu Province and Weifang in Shandong Province, and the village of Yangliuqing in the city of Tianjin, are renowned for their New Year pictures.

年畫 ■ 年畫別具一格地描繪了對福氣和幸運的憧憬，其中木刻年畫的風格最為鮮明。現代年畫均為機器印刷。東漢前即已在桃木符上雕刻門神像，這便是年畫的起源。到了宋代，其主題已演化為日常生活和社會的各個方面，包括豐收、花鳥、山水、神話故事和門神畫，也祈求福運、長壽、和婚姻的幸福。天津的楊柳青、江蘇的桃花塢、山東的濰坊都是著名的年畫產地。

lucky children / Pictures of a boy and a girl are often pasted on the exterior door of a house or business. The auspicious pair together are most commonly known as Da A Fu, and bring protection, luck, and happiness. They were originally made from clay and called 'Jiangsu Wuxi Huishan Clay Children' and are now also drawn on paper. These two plump children are popular in folk art throughout the country and are sometimes shown carrying a green lion. Newlyweds enjoy putting statues of them in their new homes.

大阿福 ■ 在中國，家庭和商店的外門經常貼著一對童男童女的年畫。這兩個胖胖的小孩有時牽著一頭綠獅子，他們就是給人們帶來保祐、福運和喜慶的大阿福。大阿福源於江蘇無錫惠山泥人，用陶土製成，後來其形象被描繪在紙上，成為流行全國的民間藝術。新婚夫婦喜歡將他們的塑像擺放在新房裡。

大阿福的傳說

在江蘇無錫惠山，住著兩只兇險的獅子，它們以捕食小孩為樂。惠山的百姓無法忍受這種殘忍和痛苦，就向神明祈禱。禱告終於傳到天上的玉皇大帝那裡，他派遣兩位神靈變成一對童男童女，下到人間，憑著他們非凡的神通和武藝，將兩只獅子降服歸順。這兩個神靈變的小孩就成了討人喜歡的大阿福，帶給人們保祐和福運，受到廣泛的崇敬。

legend of lucky children / In the Huishan hills of Wuxi, Jiangsu Province, there lived two menacing green lions that preyed upon children. The residents could not bear the atrocities and suffering any longer, so they prayed to the spirits. Word eventually reached the Jade Emperor in heaven, who dispatched two spirits to earth. The spirits transformed themselves into children, and through cunning and skill, managed to subdue the lions. These two spirit children were venerated as Da A Fu, and became widely loved as protective spirits and bringers of good fortune.

瓶 vase (*píng*) = 平安

vase / Pronounced *píng*, the vase represents peace and safety, *píng píng ān ān*, because of a play on the first character in the word 'peace,' *píng ān*. A vase presented to a friend as a gift conveys a wish for peace. A picture of a vase with flowers from all four seasons is a rebus for 'may one enjoy peace in all seasons,' *sì jié píng ān*. The word 'apple,' *píng gǔo*, sounds similar and is thus another symbol for 'peace.' During the New Year period, if a vessel is broken, the phrase *suì suì píng ān*, meaning 'peace and safety every year', is spoken to offset the bad omen, since *suì* means both 'to break' and 'year.' The vase can be found as a motif in many aspects of folk art, including paper cuts, woodcuts, stone carvings, and New Year pictures.

peace *(píng ān)*

瓶 ■ 「瓶」與「平」諧音，因此瓶代表著平安與和平，平平安安。送一個花瓶給朋友作禮物，即傳達了平安的祝願。瓶裡插著四季的花卉，寓意「四季平安」。「蘋果」這個詞也因與「平」諧音，被視作和平與平安的象徵。在新年期間，如果打碎一個花瓶，為了抵消不吉利的意思，人們將會說「歲歲平安」，因為「碎」與「歲」諧音。花瓶的圖案，廣泛地應用在中國藝術的各個方面，包括剪紙、木刻、石刻、以及年畫。

gourd / The gourd is said to embody heaven and earth, and to contain spiritual energy that wards off evil spirits. It is often hung for protection above a door or window, at the head of a bed, or in a vehicle. One of the Taoist treasures, the gourd, *hú lu*, is also a vessel for magic elixirs. Li Tie Guai, one of the Eight Immortals and a master magician, carries the gourd as his treasure.

葫蘆 ■ 相傳葫蘆能將天地均容納其中，能以靈氣驅逐邪氣，因此人們將葫蘆懸掛在門上、窗戶裡、床頭以及汽車內，以驅邪避惡。葫蘆也是道士的法寶之一，內裝神奇的萬靈藥，「八仙」之一的鐵拐李正因為有葫蘆作他的法寶，而成為魔法大師。

葫蘆的傳說

美猴王孫悟空，是十六世紀神話小說《西游記》裡著名的主角。

他偷聽到兩個小妖怪準備用神奇的紅葫蘆來捕捉他，於是他就搖身變作一名老真人，等在路邊。當小妖怪向他炫耀寶葫蘆能裝一千人時，猴王變出一個假葫蘆，宣稱他的法寶能裝天。小妖怪被這樣的法寶吸引住了，就與他討價還價，說如果他証實了他的法寶真有魔力裝天，它們就拿紅葫蘆與他交換。猴王立即與天上的神靈聯絡，求得將日月星辰遮閉半個時辰，使小妖怪相信天的確被裝進了他的假葫蘆裡，從而得意洋洋地將寶葫蘆騙到手，最終打敗了妖怪。

legend of the gourd / In the sixteenth-century novel 'Journey to the West,' the Monkey King, *Sūn Wù Kōng,* hears that the demons are on their way to capture him, using their magic gourd. Disguising himself as an immortal, he intercepts them. When the demons show him their gourd that can hold a thousand people, the Monkey King reveals a gourd he claims can hold the entire heavens. Impressed by his treasure, the demons bargain to swap with him if he can prove that his gourd really has the power to contain the sky. By obtaining permission from the spirits to block the light of the sun, moon, and stars for one hour, the Monkey King is able to fool the demons into believing he has bottled the heavens in his ordinary gourd and thus is triumphant in acquiring their magic one.

龍 ■　龍是仁慈和神秘的虛幻動物，它一直廣泛地被人們崇敬。人們相信它能帶來雨水和豐收，所以龍就成為保祐和福運的象徵。龍有神力，可以忽隱忽現，可以悠游或潛藏於天上、海底、河裡、雲霧和雨中。所以，它經常被描繪成在雲靄中遨翔。早在商朝，「龍」字就被雕刻在占卜用的甲骨上。從漢朝以來，龍的形象就被採用為皇帝和皇權威嚴的象徵，五爪金龍已專屬皇宮貴族所用。到了清朝，龍作為皇家紋章而繡在大清國旗上。一般老百姓則被禁止使用龍的圖案，往後才漸漸地重新回到民間風俗之中。

龍的顯現被視為福運的徵兆，常被認作是偉人的誕生或朝代的更替的象徵。相傳孔夫子出生前，就有龍顯現。

dragon / The dragon, *lóng*, is a benevolent and mystical creature that was once widely worshiped by the common people to bring rain and good harvests. Thus, the dragon is an auspicious symbol of protection and fortune. The dragon has power to be either visible or invisible and inhabits the skies, seas, rivers, mist, and rain. Consequently, the dragon is often depicted flying among clouds. The character *lóng* is inscribed on oracle bones dating back to the Shang dynasty (ca.1600–ca.1027 B.C.). From the Han dynasty (206 B.C.–A.D. 220) onward, the dragon was adopted as a symbol for the emperor and became a potent emblem of imperial power. The image of the five-clawed dragon was reserved for the upper ranks of the imperial palace, and in the Qing dynasty (1661–1011) the dragon became the imperial crest embroidered on the national flag. Common folk were long prohibited from using the dragon motif, though gradually it reentered the people's vernacular. The appearance of the dragon was seen as an omen of good fortune and often marked the birth of a great man or dynasty. The dragon is said to have shown itself just prior to the birth of Confucius in 551 B.C.

龍舞．獅舞 ■ 從崇拜和求雨的儀式演化而來的龍舞，是在元宵節裡驅魔祈福的傳統表演，以示新年慶會之收尾。在農曆新年期間的獅舞，也是一種十分流行的演出，不僅即將到來的一年帶來幸運和福氣，而且也創造出節日的氣氛。獅舞起源於三國時代，而廣泛流行於南北朝。

dragon and lion dances /
The dragon dance, *lóng wǔ*,
which evolved from the worship
and inducement of rain, is traditionally performed during the
Lantern Festival, which marks
the end of the New Year period.
It is thought to bring fortune
and dispel evil. Another popular
performance during New Year,
the lion dance, *shī wǔ*, not only
brings luck and fortune for the
coming year but also creates
a festive atmosphere. The lion
dance originated during the
Three Kingdoms (220–265),
and its popularity spread during
the Northern and Southern
dynasties (420–589).

scepter / The *rú yì* scepter is a short sword that symbolizes 'everything as you wish.' It is the first of the eight Buddhist treasures, and its shape is said to have been derived from the magic fungus of immortality, *líng zhī*. When given as a present, the scepter conveys wishes for good fortune and prosperity. The earliest scepters, made of iron, were used as weapons. Later versions were in gold, silver, jade, amber, porcelain, bone, or wood.

An image of the *rú yì* combined with a vase, *píng*, representing peace, forms the rebus *píng ān rú yì*, meaning 'may you have peace and everything as you wish.' When the Gods of Peace and Harmony, *Hé hé èr xiān*, are shown holding a *rú yì*, it symbolizes 'harmony and everything as you wish,' *hé hé rú yì*.

如意 ■ 如意有一切如意的含意，是一種短劍式的節杖，也是佛教八樣法寶之首。相傳它的外形起源於神秘的菌蕈類植物—靈芝，作為禮物送人，象徵著祝福和成功。最早的如意是用鐵做的，作為武器使用。後來金的、銀的、玉的、琥珀、陶瓷、骨的、木的各種樣式都有。如意和花瓶在一起組成的圖案，寓意「平安如意」。和合二仙捧著如意，則象徵「和合如意」。

如意 scepter

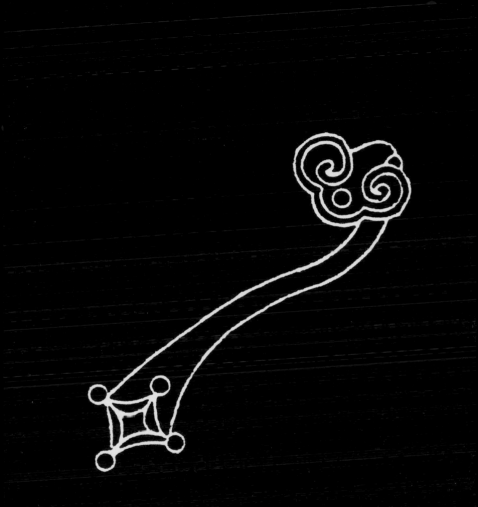

(*rú yì*) = everything as you wish

雲　■　鑒於「雲」與「運」諧音，「雲」常稱之為「祥雲」，即吉祥、幸運之意。具有代表性的是「五色雲」，象徵著「五福」。所以，雲的圖案就廣泛地應於建築、紡織品以及日常用品的設計上。雲的圖案連綿不斷，就創造出「福運無邊」的寓意。裝飾風格的雲的圖案就象神仙的靈芝和如意，不少神仙都乘雲遨遊。

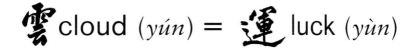

雲 cloud (*yún*) = **運** luck (*yùn*)

cloud / Because the word for 'cloud,' *yún*, and the word for 'good luck,' *yùn*, sound similar, this symbol is often referred to as the 'auspicious cloud,' *xiáng yún*. A typical auspicious cloud is five colored, *wǔ sè yún*, and represents five layers of fortune and happiness. The cloud has become a popular motif in architecture, textile designs, and everyday objects. When it is repeated in a pattern, it symbolizes never-ending fortune. The stylized rendering of the cloud motif is similar in form to the fungus of immortality, *líng zhī*, and the *rú yì* scepter. Numerous gods and immortals used the cloud as a vehicle on which they traveled.

windmill / Purchased during New Year, particularly in southern China, the windmill, or pinwheel, is said 'to turn one's luck around,' *zhuǎn yùn*, in the coming year. Windmills often feature a lucky phrase wishing good fortune, longevity, or wealth for the year ahead.

風車 ■ 在中國，特別在南方，人們相信買一架風車過年，可以在來年中轉變運氣，即轉運。風車經常被賦予幸運的語句，祝願在新的一年中好運、長壽或發財。

佛手 Buddha's hand (*fó shǒu*)

佛手 ■ 佛手即香櫞，形狀如手，充當為佛之手，「佛」與「福」諧音，因此表示「福運」之意。佛手與桃、石榴放在一起，代表福運、長壽和多子多孫。其中桃象徵「壽」，石榴象徵「生育」。由於佛手的形狀與佛的「手印」相似，所以也成為佛的象徵。

=  luck (*fú*)

buddha's hand / The finger-shaped citron known as Buddha's hand (*Citrus medica*), *fó shǒu*, stands for luck and happiness. The first character, *fó*, meaning 'Buddha,' sounds much like *fú*, the word for 'luck.' An image of a Buddha's hand together with a peach and a pomegranate signifies 'may you have an abundance of luck, longevity, and children.' The peach symbolizes longevity, the pomegranate fertility. The fruit is also a symbol of Buddhism because the upturned fingers resemble the classic position of a Buddha's hand.

shrimp / Many foods served over the New Year are considered a good omen due to their close phonetic relationship to auspicious or pleasant words. The pronunciation of the word 'shrimp,' $xi\bar{a}$ in Mandarin and ha in Cantonese, imitates the sound of laughter, thereby implying merriment and well-being.

蝦　■　在新年期間許多食品，根據其發音與吉祥詞語相諧，都被賦予了好的兆頭。象「蝦」的發音，無論粵語或國語均與笑聲相似，蝦也就成了招待客人的佳肴。

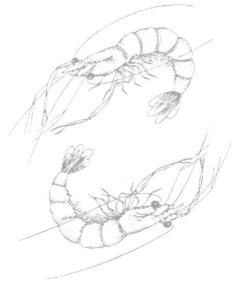

蝦 shrimp $(xi\bar{a})$ = ha ha ha

開口笑 ■ 人們經常在新年或節日吃的「開口笑」,是一種甜的,用麵粉做的,上面撒滿芝麻的南方特產。由於將麵餅割開一半,在油炸時就伸展成裂開嘴笑的樣子,所以起名「開口笑」,表示喜慶和福運。

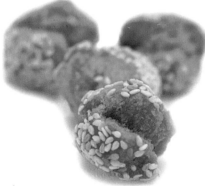

laughing mouth / *Kāi kǒu xiào* is a sweet from southern China made from dough covered with sesame seeds and is eaten at New Year and other holidays. The dough is cut halfway through, so that once it is fried, the pastry expands to resemble a laughing mouth. The name literally means 'laughing open mouth,' evoking happiness and good fortune.

籤語餅 ■ 「籤語餅」的形狀就象中國古代的錢幣—元寶。這種含有籤語的甜餅，可不是中國的土產，其實是一九二〇年左右，在三藩市的製麵廠裡發明出來的。美國的中國餐館的員工將表示好運的詞句，印在小紙條上，包入餅中，在飯後作為甜品招待客人。早期的「籤語餅」則放有孔夫子的語錄。

fortune cookie / These sweets, which enclose messages of good fortune written on small strips of paper, are not indigenous to China. Fortune cookies, *qiān yǔ bǐng*, were created by Chinese workers in a San Francisco noodle factory in the 1920s and are now given out at restaurants in the United States after a meal. The shape of the cookies is similar to that of ancient Chinese money known as *yuán bǎo*. Originally, the cookies contained sayings by Confucius.

oysters / Prepared during New Year, dried oysters bring good fortune for the upcoming year. The word for oysters, *háo*, is a pun on the phrase 'good events,' *hǎo shì*. They are often served in southern China with thin rice noodles and seaweed, *fā cái*.

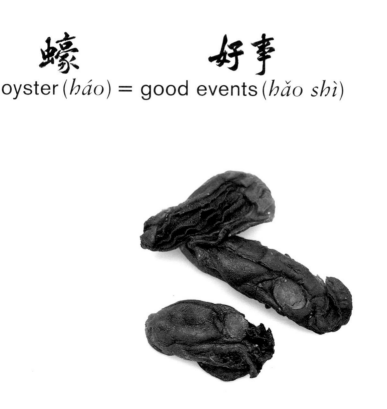

蠔　好事

oyster (*háo*) = good events (*hǎo shì*)

蠔　■　農曆新年必備的年貨—蠔豉，被認為能給新的一年帶來好運，因為「蠔豉」與「好事」諧音，所以蠔豉就常常與發菜、粉絲放一起，成為佳肴。

prosperity

The second element of the five-fold happinesses—prosperity, or *lù*—embodies status, honor, and advancement to high office. *Lù* literally means 'official salary.' Great importance was placed upon education because anyone who passed the imperial examinations received the honor of becoming a public official.

Achieving this high rank guaranteed an affluent and fortunate life. *Lù* differs from the fifth element of happiness, *cái,* or 'wealth,' because *cái* refers to wealth acquired through business. Symbols for *lù* include the deer, the carp leaping over the dragon's gate, the peony, the monkey, and the God of Prosperity.

「五福」之二的「祿」，原意為官吏的職位和俸給，包含地位、功名以及加官進爵。官位的高低是以教育程度來決定的，任何人只要通過皇家的科舉會考，取得功名，就成為朝廷官員。搏得高階位就意味著有了富裕和幸福生活的保証。這個「祿」，與本書中「五福」之五的「財」略有不同，因為「財」講得是經商賺來的財富。「祿」的象徵形象，包括鹿、鯉魚跳龍門、牡丹、猴以及祿神。

A folk game which reflects people's desire for status.
民間游戲《升官圖》反映出人們對升官發財的渴望。

鹿 deer (*lù*) = 祿 prosperity (*lù*)

鹿 ■ 「鹿」與「祿」諧音，常被賦予「祿神」的寓意，一百隻鹿代表「百祿」。由於相傳鹿能活千年以上，所以鹿也成為長壽的象徵。鹿常常伴隨著祿神出現，還被信奉為唯一能找到靈芝仙草的動物。同時，鹿和鶴也都是靈芝仙草的護衛者。

deer / The word 'deer' is pronounced identically to the word for prosperity, *lù*, and is often employed in rebuses to stand for the God of Prosperity, *Lù xīng*. One hundred deer represent 'prosperity one hundred times over,' *bǎi lù*. Because the deer is said to live over a thousand years, it is also an emblem of long life. The God of Longevity is often accompanied by the deer, believed to be the only creature that can find the magic fungus of immortality, *líng zhī*. The deer and the crane are both guardians of this sacred fungus.

deer / The deer is often mentioned in ancient texts such as the Confucius classic 'Book of Poetry,' *Shī jīng*, a collection of more than three hundred poems and songs from the middle years of the Zhou dynasty (ca.1027–256 B.C.). A picture of a deer in combination with the characters for 'luck' and 'longevity' creates one of the most propitious messages for the Chinese—'luck, prosperity, and longevity,' *fú, lù, shòu*.

The deer is also associated with sovereignty. *Zhú lù zhōng yuán*, literally 'to chase the deer to the central plains,' expresses the idea of seizing control of an empire. *Lù sǐ shuí shǒu* means 'at whose hands shall the deer die?' and asks who shall gain supremacy.

鹿 ■ 古代史料例如孔子編撰的《詩經》中就經常提到鹿。鹿的圖案，和中文的「福」與「壽」組合在一起，創造出寓意最為吉祥的象徵符號—福、祿、壽。

鹿也與皇權帝位的追逐連在一起，例如用「逐鹿中原」以表達統合整個帝國的雄心。「鹿死誰手」則表示誰能贏得霸權。

祿神 ■ 祿神，是福、祿、壽三星神之一。人們年深月久地崇敬這三星神，相信他們執掌著人生天命的答案。「祿星高照」的祝詞，反映了人們對祿星的信仰。後來，祿星演化成穿著官袍、手執如意的神明。祿神被認為可以給人帶來成功的生涯。

god of prosperity / *Lù xīng*, the God of Prosperity, is one of the three stellar gods—along with the God of Luck and the God of Longevity. Historically, people worshiped the three as stars, believing they held the key to life's destiny. The phrase 'the prosperity star watches over you,' *lù xīng gāo zhào*, reflects people's veneration of the star. The prosperity star was thought to govern a person's success in a career. Later, the star was transformed into a deity wearing an official's robe and carrying the *rú yì* scepter.

祿神 ■ 在傳統戲台上，祿神總是第一個出場表演，以升官發財來祝福觀眾。這種程式有時在中國戲曲正式演出前仍可看到。祿神表演者面戴白色的「加官臉」，穿大紅袍，手執朝笏，繞場三週，笑而不言，退場。再次進場，手抱一兒，繞場三週，退場。最後出場時，他滿面笑容，並展開手中的紅色條幅，上面寫著「加官進祿」的頌詞。

god of prosperity /
Theatrical performances were traditionally preceded by an act featuring the God of Prosperity. His appearance on stage blesses the audience with prosperity. The act is sometimes still performed prior to traditional Chinese operas and plays. Wearing a white mask and a red robe and holding a tablet, the actor circles the stage three times, laughing without saying a word. He enters a second time, carrying a child, and again circles the stage three times. On the third entrance, he reveals a scroll inscribed with the words 'the more promotion, the more salary,' *jiā guān jìn lù*.

鯉魚跳龍門 ■ 根據傳說，鯉魚每年一次會逆流而上，去黃河上游產卵，跳過龍門瀑布者，便化為龍。自從宋朝以來，「鯉魚跳龍門」的諺語就有科舉及第、功成名就的隱喻。科舉制度在漢朝即已建立，目的是選擇頂尖的學者來擔當最高朝廷官員。後來科舉會考向一般民眾開放，允許任何人只要通過會考成為朝廷官員，就能保證有特權的生活，給全家帶來財富和榮耀。「鯉」與「利」相諧音，所以有利益、優惠之含意。

carp leaping over the dragon's gate / Each year, according to legend, carp swam the Yellow River upstream to spawn, and those able to leap the waterfall at the dragon's gate, *lóng mén*, were transformed into dragons. Since the Song dynasty (960–1279), the phrase 'carp leaping over the dragon's gate turning into a dragon,' *lĭ yú tiào lóng mén*, has been used as a metaphor for success in passing the imperial examinations.

The exams were established in the Han dynasty (206 B.C.–A.D. 220) to select the best scholars for the highest government positions. Later the tests were open to the general public and anyone who passed would become a government official, ensuring a life of privilege, wealth, and prestige for the entire family. The words for 'carp,' *lĭ*, and 'profit,' *lì*, are identical apart from tone; thus the carp symbolizes a wish for benefits and advantage.

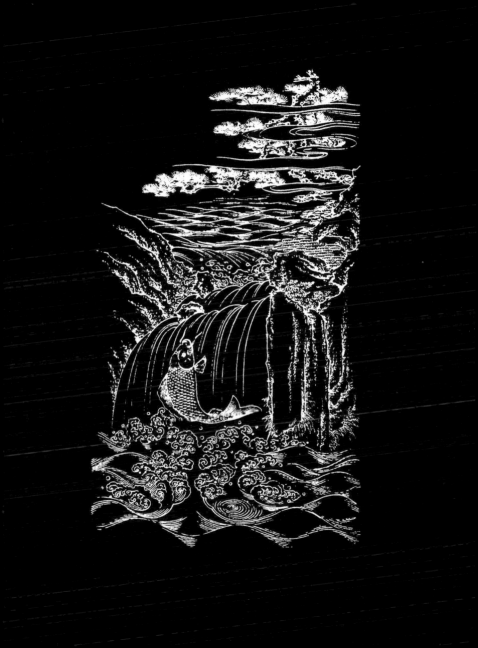

六 six *(liù)* = 祿 prosperity *(lù)*

「六」字 ■ 「六」字的發音與「祿」相似，所以也象徵官位和晉升。

「六六大順」是流行極廣的成語，表述生活中事事順利的祝願。所以一個月中的第六天，就被看作為開張營業、生孩子、舉行婚禮或其它慶賀的吉日。送禮時，「六」便是吉數，例如送六瓶酒、十六只橙子、十六盎司等。由於中國有著眾多的方言，「六」在某些地方卻是不吉利的，例如在湖北，「六」字則與「死亡」相關聯。

six / The number six, *liù*, sounds similar to *lù*, 'prosperity,' and thus is a symbol for rank and promotion. Six signifies everything in life flowing smoothly: the popular saying *liù liù dà shùn* means 'everything goes smoothly with six.' The sixth day of the month is considered a lucky day to open a business, give birth, or hold a wedding or other celebration. A gift consisting of several identical items or a quantity of wine, oranges, or tea, for example, is considered lucky if the total contains the number six: six bottles, sixteen oranges, sixteen ounces. Because China has many dialects and cultural variations, six is considered unlucky in some areas, such as Hubei Province, where it resembles a word for death.

牡丹 ■ 牡丹，象徵著富貴，而被中國人尊崇為最高貴的花卉。自隋唐時代起，牡丹便在皇宮花苑中大受歡迎，並被賦予「花王」和「富貴花」之稱。其中黃色和紫色的牡丹價值最高。牡丹也象徵春天，並且被用來隱喻美人。

瓶中插著牡丹的圖案，是祝你「富貴平安」，因為牡丹代表富貴，瓶寓意平安。玉蘭、海棠和牡丹合在一起，表達「玉堂富貴」的祝願。牡丹和荷、菊、梅一起盛開的圖案，象徵「四季平安」。

peony / Esteemed as one of the most exquisite flowers, the peony, *mǔ dan*, is a symbol for prosperity and nobility, *fù guì*. The peony became popular in the imperial palaces during the Sui and Tang dynasties (581–907), and thus earned the titles 'king of flowers,' *huā wáng*, and the 'flower of wealth, rank, and honor,' *fù guì huā*. The yellow and purple varieties are considered to be of the highest value. The peony also symbolizes spring and is used as a metaphor for female beauty.

The image of a peony in a vase expresses the wish for 'prosperity and peace,' *fù guì píng ān*, because the vase is a rebus for 'peace,' *píng ān*. The combination of a peony, a magnolia, and a Chinese crab-apple flower stands for 'wealth and high rank,' *yú táng fù guì*. Pictured with a lotus, chrysanthemum, and plum blossom, the peony symbolizes 'peace and fortune in the four seasons,' *sì jì píng ān*.

猴 ■ 「猴」與侯爵的「侯」同音雙關，表示名與權俱有，祝願榮達。一隻猴子騎在馬上的圖畫，強有力地傳達出「馬上封侯」的信息，因為「馬上」為「立即」之意。一隻猴子伸手摘取掛在楓樹上黃金印，其吉祥意義是「封侯掛印」，「楓」與「封」諧音，寓意顯赫權貴。

monkey / The word for 'monkey,' *hóu*, is pronounced the same as the word for 'high-ranking official,' *hóu*, and therefore represents a wish for advancement and prosperity. The well-known image of a monkey riding a horse is a message for 'quick advancement to high position,' *mǎ shàng fēng hóu*. The horse, *mǎ*, is a rebus for the word 'immediately' or 'quickly,' *mǎ shàng*. A picture of a monkey reaching for a royal seal hanging from the branch of a tree expresses the wish that one will attain a high position in the royal court, *fēng hóu guà yìn*.

三元 ■ 元寶，即帽狀的金錠、銀錠，在中國古代用作為錢幣，也象徵著財富和成功。那些通過古代科舉三試、名列榜首的讀書人，稱為「三元」——解元、會元、狀元。由於元寶有「元」字，所以三個元寶即寓意「三元」，作為功成名就的有力象徵。荔枝、桂圓和核桃組合在一起，由於其圓形與「元」同音，也代表「三元」。

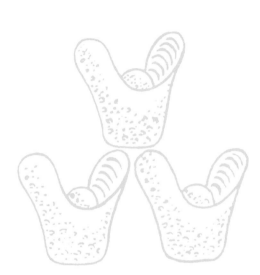

three ingots / A popular symbol of prosperity, *yuán bǎo* are hat-shaped gold and silver ingots used as money in ancient China. Scholars who passed the imperial examinations with the highest marks were referred to as *jiě yuán*, *huì yuán*, and *zhuàng yuán*, collectively referred to as the 'three yuans.' Because the word for ingots also contains *yuán*, a picture of three ingots creates a rebus for the 'three yuans,' *sān yuán*, making it a symbol of status and honor. The lichee, longan, and walnut in combination also represent the 'three yuans,' as they are all round in shape, and the word for 'round' is pronounced *yuán*.

rooster / A picture of a rooster and a cockscomb flower conveys a wish for advancement. This is because the rooster's crest, *guān*, is a pun on a word meaning both an 'official' and an 'official's hat,' *guān*. Combined with the cockscomb flower, *jī guān huā*, it forms a double pun, creating the phrase 'promotion upon promotion,' *guān shàng jiā guān*. The rooster is also seen as an auspicious creature that can ward off evil spirits. A heavenly rooster lived in the peach tree on Dusu Mountain that was guarded by Shen Tu and Yu Lei. When the heavenly rooster crowed, all the other roosters on earth would follow suit, scaring the evil spirits away.

雄雞 ■ 畫一雄雞立於雞冠花前，寓意官運亨通、連連升遷。因為雞冠花與雄雞皆有冠，「冠」與「官」同音同義，傳達了「官上加官」的祝願。雄雞也是能驅鬼避邪的吉祥物，而大受歡迎。由神荼和郁壘守衛的度朔山上，就有一隻天雞棲息在大桃樹上，每當日出天雞啼叫時，天下所有的雄雞都隨著啼叫起來，將不祥之鬼魅趕走。

蟹　■　蟹同樣代表功名富貴。因為蟹有甲，中國古代科舉制度的殿試有三甲之分，兩隻蟹代表一甲、二甲，為會試之最高等級。

crab ／ The crab represents prosperity and status because the word referring to its shell, *jiǎ*, is a pun on the highest level one can attain in the imperial examinations—first *jiǎ*. Two crabs represent first and second *jiǎ*.

sticky rice cake / *Nián gāo* is a steamed sticky rice cake commonly eaten during New Year festivities. The word for cake, *gāo*, is pronounced identically to 'high,' *gāo*, and when preceded by *nián*, mean-ing 'year,' it symbolizes a rise in rank or prosperity year after year. Red dates, *zǎo*, are often added to the cake to give the additional meaning of attaining high position 'early,' or *zǎo*.

年糕 ■ 年糕，即黏米做的蒸黏糕，是新年必備之食品。「糕」諧音「高」，取步步登高之意，而年糕則象徵一年更比一年強。年糕上也通常加放紅棗，「棗」與「早」諧音，取早日高升之意。

longevity

Longevity is the most highly esteemed value of the five-fold happinesses. The desire for long life is embodied in traditions such as eating longevity noodles and peaches on an elder's birthday. Wishes for longevity are often inscribed on scrolls displayed in homes: 'life as long as the Southern Mountain,' *shòu bǐ nán shān,* 'ten thousand long lives without end,' *wàn shòu wú jiàng,* and 'life as long as the tortoise and crane,' *guī líng hè shòu.*

Expressions of the desire for longevity can be traced back as far as the Shang and Zhou dynasties (1600–256 B.C.), with phrases such as *wàn shòu,* 'ten thousand lives,' and *jūn zǐ wàn nián*, meaning 'nobility and ten thousand years.' The word for longevity, *shòu,* has been found engraved on bronze from the Zhou dynasty (ca. 1027–256 B.C.). Respect for elders, an important Chinese virtue, is documented in texts in the Warring States

period (480 – 221 B.C.). According to Confucian thought, moral conduct was essential to living a long life, as conveyed in the saying 'compassion brings longevity, immorality brings early death.' Symbols representing the wish for longevity include the peach, the pine tree, the crane, the fungus of immortality, the God of Longevity, and the Queen Mother of the West.

松樹、鶴、靈芝、西王母以及壽神。

，惡者夭」。表現「壽」的象徵，包括了桃子、

「五福壽為先」，渴望長壽是始終被人們關注的傳統話題。例如，在慶賀老年人壽辰時，吃長壽麵和壽桃，就成為祝願長壽的有力象徵。祝壽的詞句，經常被書寫成卷軸，懸掛於家中，象「壽比南山」、「萬壽無疆」以及「龜齡鶴壽」等。這種祈求長壽的表達，可以追溯到商周時代。

早在商朝，「萬壽」的觀念就已出現。在周朝的青銅器的銘文上，經常可以看到「壽」字。尊老敬老，一向是中國人極為推崇的傳統美德，早在戰國時代的史料中就有記載。孔夫子認為，道德是長壽的必要條件，所以他說：「仁者壽

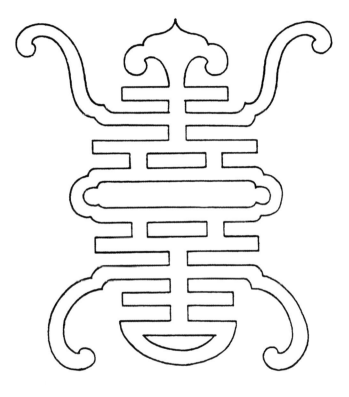

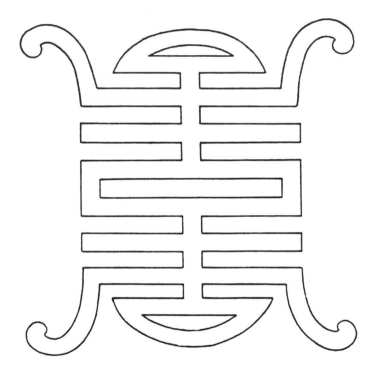

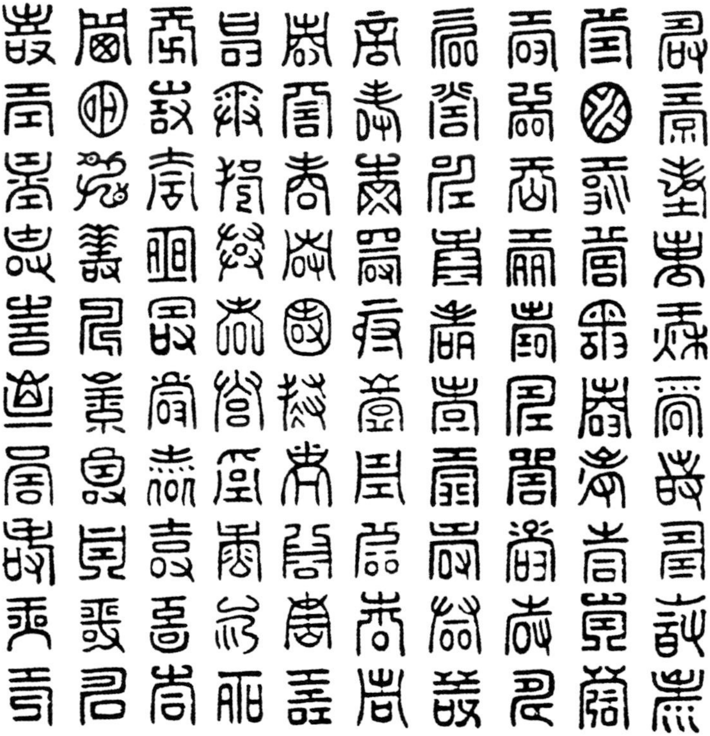

《百壽圖》 ■ 在中國古代生活中，長壽是人生價值觀的核心。所以，中國書法家創造出眾多不同的書體，來表現「壽」的主題。用篆書寫一百個不同形狀的「壽」字，即組成《百壽圖》，是經常用來送給老年人的壽禮之一。

one hundred long lives / In ancient China, the wish for longevity became one of the most central values of life. Chinese calligraphers developed numerous styles to express the character in written form. When inscribed one hundred times in varying calligraphic styles, the word 'longevity,' *shòu*, becomes the motif known as *bǎi shòu*, 'a hundred long lives.' The motif is often sent as a gift to elders to wish them long life.

god of longevity / *Shòu xīng*, the God of Longevity, is the most popular of the three stellar gods, outshining the God of Luck and the God of Prosperity. His name literally means 'longevity star.' The image of the God of Longevity is well known today: he is a benevolent old gentleman with a smiling face and a prominent forehead who holds a dragon-headed walking stick in one hand and the peach of immortality in the other. Legend has it that the God of Longevity began as the star Canopus in the southern constellation Argo, also known as the Old Man of the South Pole. People worshiped this and other stars in the belief that the heavens ruled human fate. 'Records of the Historian,' *Shǐ jì*, an important document of China's history written during the Han dynasty (206 B.C.–A.D. 220), states, 'peace prevails in the world when the Old Man of the South Pole appears; when he is not present, there is cause for great concern.'

壽神 ■ 壽神是福、祿、壽三星神中最有影響的一位。壽神即壽星。如今，壽星的形象家喻戶曉，是一位長頭高額、慈眉善目的白髮老翁，一手拄著龍頭拐杖，一手托著仙桃。相傳壽神源於二十八宿東方蒼龍七宿中的角亢二宿，也有人認為是南極的老人星。古人崇拜星宿，相信占星術能測定人生的命運。漢代司馬遷所寫的經典史書《史記‧天官書》記載：「老人（星）見，治安；不見，兵起。」

god of longevity / In the Eastern Han dynasty (25–220), worship of the God of Longevity was combined with ceremonies to honor elders. One such ritual was to bestow on persons over the age of seventy a nine-foot-long jade walking stick. It is from this period on that the God of Longevity began carrying his dragon-headed walking stick.

During the Zhou and Qin dynasties (1027–206 B.C.), shrines were built in honor of the God of Longevity, and the first emperor of China, Qin Shi Huangdi, from the Qin dynasty, was said to have offered sacrifices to him. By the Ming dynasty (1368–1644), the belief in the God of Longevity had become widespread, although his worship no longer centered in shrines.

壽神 ■ 在東漢時，祭祀老人星的儀式與尊老敬老結合起來，對全國進入古稀之年（七十歲）的老人，「授之以王杖」，即一根九尺長，上端飾以鳩頭的拐杖。壽星手持的龍頭拐杖即源於此。

在周秦之際，已特置祭壇祭祀壽神。傳說中國第一帝—秦始皇也要給壽神供獻牲禮。到了明代，雖然再也沒有特置壽神壇，然而對壽神的信仰已經廣為流傳。

壽神的傳說

在明代著名戲劇《白蛇傳》裡，白蛇變作一個美人，與忠厚的許仙相愛而結合。一天，她因飲雄黃酒而現出原形，許仙驚嚇而死。白蛇乃潛入昆侖山，想盜取靈芝仙草，以救其丈夫性命。不幸，她被守衛靈芝仙草的鶴、鹿二仙童打敗。壽星仙翁對其遭遇十分同情，憐而以靈芝仙草相贈，從而救活許仙。

legend of the god of longevity / In 'Collection of White Snake,' *Bái shé zhuàn*, from the Ming dynasty (1368–1644), which has since become a popular play, Lady White Snake takes the form of a beautiful woman who falls in love and marries a mortal man, Xu Xian. One day she drinks wine laced with an alchemical substance that brings out her true nature as a snake, and she frightens Xu Xian to death. White Snake secretly races off to Kunlun Mountain to steal the sacred fungus of immortality, *líng zhī xiān cǎo*, which can bring him back to life. Unfortunately, she is defeated in battle by two spirits guarding the magic fungus. The God of Longevity, seeing her misfortune, takes pity on her and presents her the fungus of immortality as a gift, restoring her husband's life.

legend of the god of longevity / The ancient text 'Records of Seeking Immortals,' *Sōu shén jì*, tells the story of a nineteen-year-old boy, Yan Chao, who meets a sage and learns that he is destined to die the next day. Yan Chao pleads for his life, but the sage replies that it is not in his power to change fate and urges him to go home to inform his parents. On hearing the news, his parents seek out the sage and beg him to help their son. The sage advises them to prepare some venison and wine for Yan Chao to deliver to two men who will be playing chess under a mulberry tree on their property the next day. He warns that Yan Chao should not say a word under any circumstances. The next day, Yan Chao discovers the men under the tree, just as the sage predicted. They are so engrossed in their chess game that they do not notice at first who has provided them with their meat and wine. A few games later, they catch sight of Yan Chao and realize that they have consumed all his offerings. They decide to repay his generosity by altering the Register of Destiny, though the man to the north comments that it is not such an easy task. The man to the south, on inspecting the Register more closely, exclaims that it can be modified easily. He takes out a brush and changes nineteen years to ninety-one years. Yan Chao returns home and lives to the ripe old age of ninety-one. The two men are said to have been the stars of the South and North Poles, who govern life and death—the South Pole star who governs life is the God of Longevity.

壽神的傳說

六朝小說《搜神記》（晉·干寶著）中記載一個關於壽神的故事：有一個名叫顏超的青年，才十九歲。一天，他在路上遇見被稱為神算的管輅，管輅算出顏超只能活到明日中午，顏超跪下叩頭，乞求救命。但是，管輅回答他說：「命在於天，我無法掌管，你還是快去告訴你父母吧。」顏超之父母得知以後，趕緊策馬追上管輅，苦苦哀求。管輅出了個主意，讓他們回去準備一盒鹿脯，一壺清酒，卯日那天讓顏超送到他們家麥地南頭的大桑樹樹下，那裡有兩個人在下棋。並警告顏超，不管出現什麼情況，他都不能說一句話。第二天，顏超果然見到兩個人在樹下，全神貫注地下棋。兩人專心致志，只顧磕頭，全然沒有注意到是誰送來酒和肉。幾盤棋之後，兩人才發現顏超跪於一旁，但坐在北邊的人說，更改命冊可不是容易的事。於是，他們想酬謝顏超慷慨的供應，但坐在北邊的人說，更改命冊可不是容易的事。坐在南邊的人拿過命冊，仔細審查之後說：「這很容易改嘛！」馬上取筆一勾，將「十九」改成了「九十」。顏超拜謝而回。管輅告訴他，那兩個人就是南斗星和北斗星，南斗主生，北斗主死，顏超可以活到九十歲。從此，這南極星就成為壽神了。

松 ■ 作為長青之木，松樹在嚴寒之中乃堅挺耐久，是朝野普遍珍視的吉祥物。多少朝代以來，在中國山水畫藝術中，松樹是畫家們最喜歡描繪的傳統主題。畫中松經常與鶴相伴在一起，因為人們認為兩者都能壽過千年，有「鶴壽松齡」之說。著名的吉祥語還有「松菊延年」和「不老松」。由於松樹的針葉成對而生，所以松樹也象徵婚姻幸福。松樹也常被種植在墳墓旁，以保護死者，因為人們相信，神話中的妖怪「罔象」，會吞食死者的腦子，卻害怕松樹。

pine tree / One of the most popular emblems of longevity, this evergreen is known for its endurance and hardiness even through the bitterest winters. Throughout the centuries, it has been the tree most favored by Chinese painters in traditional ink landscape paintings. The pine is frequently paired with the crane because they both live to a ripe age. Common sayings include 'the ageless pine,' *bù lǎo sōng*, and 'the pine and chrysanthemum extend long life,' *sōng jú yán nián*. Pine needles are a symbol of a happy marriage because they grow in pairs. Pine trees also serve a protective function when planted close to graves, since the mythical creature Wang Xiang, who devours the brains of the dead, is afraid of the pine.

松樹的傳說

人們還相信松脂有藥效，服之能防止衰老、延年益壽。傳說有一個名叫趙瞿的人，患癩病多年，病重垂死，其家人只能把他遺棄在山穴裡。不久，剛好有一位仙人路過，很可憐他，就留下一囊藥給他。趙瞿連服了一百多天，身上的毒瘡奇跡般地痊癒了，變得肌膚玉澤。當仙人再經過時，趙瞿立即跪倒，感謝救命之恩，並乞求其方。仙人解釋說，這藥是用松脂提煉精製而成的，吃了可以長生不老。趙瞿回家後經常服用松脂，活了一百多歲，齒不落，髮不白。

legend of the pine tree / A man named Zhao Qu suffered a serious illness for many years. When he was close to death, his family left him in the mountains to die. Not long after, an immortal who crossed his path took pity on him, and offered him some medicine. Zhao Qu took the medicine for one hundred days and made a miraculous recovery. His vitality returned and his skin took on a healthy glow. When the immortal passed by again, Zhao Qu dropped to his knees in heartfelt gratitude and asked what had been used to make the concoction. The immortal explained that the medicine contained pine oil. Zhao Qu went home and lived to be over a hundred years old. His teeth never fell out and his hair never turned white, and consequently pine oil is said to have medicinal qualities that prevent aging and prolong life.

竹　■　青翠挺拔，臨霜不凋，竹象徵著在逆境和惡運中不屈服的勇敢精神
。古人曾稱竹為「不剛不柔，非草非木」。由於松和竹均四時長茂，而梅
在寒冬裡盛開，所以將松、竹、梅合成一組就構成「歲寒三友」之意境。
自宋代以來，這「歲寒三友」普遍出現在陶瓷上。由於竹心空虛，所以也
象徵著謙虛之美德。

bamboo / Known for its durability and resilience through all the seasons, bamboo, which never loses its leaves, is a symbol for longevity and for courage in the midst of adversity. In ancient times, it was described as 'not stiff, not soft, not grass, and not wood.'

Bamboo, pine, and plum form a group known as 'the three friends,' since the pine and bamboo flourish year-round and the plum tree blossoms in winter. From the Song dynasty (960–1279) onward, the 'three friends' motif has been commonly used on ceramics. Because bamboo has a hollow center, and *kōng xū*, 'hollow,' sounds like *qiān xū*, 'modesty,' bamboo is also said to embody the value of modesty.

竹 ■ 點火爆竹，可以製造出象炮仗一樣的爆裂聲，因此遠古時代的人就「燃真竹以取其聲」，用來驅鬼避邪。後來，在中國新年和其它節日裡，竹子成為除邪惡保平安之吉祥物。因為「竹」與「祝」諧音，所以，畫兒童們點燃爆竹的《竹報平安》之圖案，則表達健康平安、喜慶吉利之意。

bamboo / Lighting a stick of bamboo creates a loud crackling similar to the sound of firecrackers. At one time, bamboo was burned to frighten evil spirits. Later, for New Year and other festivals, bamboo became synonymous with bringing peace. A picture of a boy lighting firecrackers is a rebus for 'wishing one peace,' *zhú bào píng ān*, because 'bamboo' is a pun on 'wish,' *zhù*.

plum / The prince of all flowers, the plum has long been held in high esteem for its beauty and also because it is one of the few flowers that blossoms in the cold of winter, making it an emblem of longevity. The plum blossom has a jadelike translucent whiteness and is often used as a metaphor for an innocent and pure woman. In ancient times, plum-colored makeup, *méi huā zhuāng*, was considered the most exquisite, and only women of great stature wore it. When the plum blossom and bamboo appear together, they create a wish for 'double happiness,' *zhú méi shuāng xǐ*, and this combination is often given as a wedding gift.

梅 ■ 人們將梅高度評價為「花中王子」，不僅因為「稟天質之至美」，而且「凌歲寒而獨開」，所以也被尊為長壽的象徵。梅花盛開時，韻逸香清、冰肌玉骨，由此經常用來比喻純潔高尚的女子。古代的「梅花妝」被公認為最精緻的粉妝，只有純潔高貴的婦女才配妝扮。當竹與盛開的梅花合在一起，就構成《竹梅雙喜》的圖案，表達「雙喜」之祝願。

cypress / The word for 'cypress,' *bǎi*, is pronounced identically to the word for 'one hundred,' *bǎi*, which symbolizes longevity; *bǎi* also sounds similar to 'generation,' *bèi*. The cypress is most commonly paired with the pine and expresses 'the pine and cypress wish you infinite youth,' *sōng bǎi cháng qīng*. Like the pine, the cypress is planted near graves to ward off evil spirits and bring protection and peace.

When paired with a persimmon, it represents 'everything as you wish in one hundred things,' *bǎi shì rú yì*, because persimmon, *shì*, sounds identical to 'things' and cypress stands for one hundred.

柏 ■ 「柏」與「百」諧音，使人聯想到百歲。「柏」也與「輩」發音相近，也與長壽相聯。柏樹總是與松樹相伴在一起，寓意「松柏長青」。由於柏樹與松樹一樣，能存活相當久，所以經常被種植在墳墓旁，以避邪保安。柏樹與柿子在一起的圖案，表示「百事如意」，因為「柿」與「事」諧音。

柏 cypress (*bǎi*) =

百 one hundred (*bǎi*)

鶴 ■ 白鶴細頸長腳，是臨於絕種的羽禽。由於其「壽不可量」，所以被視為長壽之王。許多傳說中，神仙駕鶴翔雲，鶴則被認為能載負死者的靈魂升天。鶴常被畫成站在松樹下，具有仙風道骨，象徵生命不朽，成為吉祥的組合「鶴壽松齡」。鶴與龜同為長壽祥瑞之禽，因此畫在一起，構成「龜鶴齊齡」的祝願。鶴立潮頭岩石之上，舉頭迎向太陽，寓「一品當朝」之意。因為鶴有「一品鳥」之稱，而「潮」與「朝」同音，比喻高升、掌管國家大政。

crane / A nearly extinct bird with long legs and a slender neck, the white crane is an ancient symbol for longevity because of its exceptionally long life span. In many legends the spirits ride on cranes, which are also said to bear the souls of the departed to the heavens. Believed to be immortal, cranes are frequently portrayed standing beneath a pine tree, a symbol of longevity, creating the auspicious combination *hè shòu sōng líng*, meaning 'life as long as that of the crane and the pine.' An image of the crane paired with the tortoise, another creature blessed with a long life, wishes one 'life as long as that of the crane and the tortoise,' *guī hè qí líng*. The crane standing on a rock in the incoming tide and looking at the sun signifies the wish that one may rise to high office, as the word for 'tide,' *cháo*, is pronounced the same as 'royal court,' *cháo*.

鶴的傳說

各種各樣的傳說都講到，「由人化鶴」標誌著成就「凡人登仙」、長生不死的功業。六朝小說《搜神記》（晉·干寶著）中記載：公元二世紀，遼東丁令威隱居靈虛山，修煉金丹術，得道成仙，一千年之後，化為白鶴，飛歸故里。看到遼東城門，他一面在空中徘徊，一面吟道：「有鳥有鳥丁令威，去家千年今始回，城郭如故人民非，何不學仙去，空伴冢累累。」隨後，丁令威升天而去。這個道士的故事則經由這首歌流傳下來。

legend of the crane / In various legends, humans have been transformed into cranes, indicating the attainment of eternal life. 'Records of Seeking Immortals,' *Sōu shén jì,* written in the Jin dynasty (265–420), relates a story from the second century concerning Ding Ling Wei, who retreats to Pure Spirit Mountain, *Líng xū,* to study alchemy. A thousand years later, he achieves immortality, becomes a white crane, and flies back to his hometown. On arriving, he perches near the city gates singing, 'There was once a bird named Ding Ling Wei, who returned home after a thousand years. The city walls remained, but the people had disappeared. Who wouldn't rather be immortal than perish?' Ding Ling Wei then flew to heaven. This Taoist story spread through his song.

tortoise / A spiritual creature, the tortoise conceals the secrets of the universe. Its shell was once an important medium in divination, and the first Chinese characters have been discovered inscribed on its surface. A tortoise's shell is naturally divided into twenty-four sections, which correspond to the twenty-four solar terms of the lunar calender. Due to the creature's long life and ability to endure hunger and thirst, the term 'tortoise years,' *guī líng*, is a metaphor for long life. The tortoise is often paired with the crane in auspicious pictures to wish one a long life, such as 'the tortoise and crane extend long life,' *guī hè yán nián*. Pan Gu, the creator of the universe in Chinese mythology, was attended by a tortoise.

龜 ■ 中國人相信，龜是隱藏著宇宙間秘密的靈物，因此龜甲成為占卜的靈媒。人們發現，最早的中國文字就刻在龜甲上。龜甲上自然分割的二十四板塊，與農曆的二十四個節氣相一致。龜能忍饑渴，壽命極長，因此成了長壽的象徵，「龜齡」即比喻人之長壽。龜與鶴經常被畫在一起，構成《龜齡鶴壽》、《龜鶴延年》的吉祥圖像。中國神話中開天闢地的盤古，正是由神龜伴隨而來，降臨於世。

桃 ■ 用桃來象徵長壽，源於兩千年之前。壽桃是麵粉做成的桃形蒸包，以紅豆、棗泥、蓮子為餡。在老年人誕辰時，經常用蒸麵桃來招待客人，以祝福長壽、健康。桃果不僅具有文化意義，而且桃木和桃花也都具有象徵意義。人們相信，惡鬼邪魔害怕桃木，所以桃符經常被懸掛在門外，以驅魔祛邪。門神像也曾被畫在兩塊桃木板上，而桃核則被雕刻成小小的避邪護身符，送給小孩佩帶，以保長命。桃花象徵春天和美人的比擬，在古典詩文中比比皆是。

peach / Use of the peach as a symbol of longevity originated over two thousand years ago. 'Longevity peaches' are steamed buns made of dough shaped like a peach and filled with red bean, date, or lotus-seed paste. The buns are served at an elder's birthday to wish long life and good health for many years to come. Not only the fruit but also the wood and blossoms of the peach tree are symbolic. Bad spirits feared peachwood and so peachwood charms were often hung outside doors or gates to keep them away. Door gods would be engraved or drawn on peach-wood, or only their names would be written on peach-wood. Peach pits were carved into little amulets and given to children to protect them and ensure long life. Classical poems and texts often mention peach blossoms as metaphors for springtime and beauty.

legends of the peach / In the Ming dynasty novel 'Journey to the West,' the mischievous Monkey King, *Sūn Wù Kōng*, achieved eternal life by stealing the peaches of immortality from the garden belonging to the Queen Mother of the West just before she held the famous 'Banquet of the Peaches,' *pán táo huì*, for all the immortals. The magic peach tree takes three thousand years to blossom and the fruits ripen in another three thousand years. Offended that he had not been invited to the banquet, the Monkey King cast a spell on the servants, allowing him to consume the exotic food and wine before the guests arrived. Drunk from the wine, he lost his way back to his heavenly abode and came upon the palace of the Supreme Lord Tao, *Tài Shàng Lǎo Jūn*, where the pills of immortality were kept. Excited at finding the immortals' most valued treasure, the Monkey King swallowed all the pills in one go—attaining double immortality, since the peaches had given him immortality earlier.

According to ancient texts, the Queen Mother of the West once descended to earth and gave four peaches of immortality, each granting six hundred years of life, to Emperor Wu Di of the Western Han dynasty (206 B.C.–A.D. 8). After eating them, he kept the peach pits, intending to grow the fruits himself and achieve eternal life. But he was then informed by the Queen Mother that the peaches are unable to grow on earth, as the soil is not fertile enough to sustain the tree for six hundred years, until the fruit is ripe. Since then, eating peaches has come to represent a wish for long life.

桃的傳說

在明代古典傳奇小說《西游記》中，仙桃樹三千年開花，三千年結實，食一枚可增壽六百年。王母娘娘正準備為眾神仙舉行聞名的「蟠桃宴會」，卻被淘氣的孫悟空事先在花園裡把仙桃偷吃了。孫悟空氣不過沒有被邀請去赴宴，就念聲咒語，將來摘桃的仙女們定身那裡，獨自去赴宴，並在眾神仙未到之時，將仙果、仙酒吃個精光。他醉酒之後，把回齊天府之路走差了，卻來到太上老君的兜率天宮，發現那裡藏有長生不死之金丹靈藥，此物乃仙家至寶。猴子得之大喜，一下子將所有的金丹丸吞下。加上先前偷吃仙桃，他加倍地煉就了不朽的生命。

相傳二千多年前，西王母率眾仙女下凡游覽，給漢武帝帶來四枚仙桃，每顆仙桃可延壽六百年。漢武帝「食桃輒以核著膝前」，想日後親自種植，以求長生不朽。西王母笑道：「此桃三千年一生實耳。中夏地薄，種之不生也。」自此，吃桃就成為祝願長壽的象徵。

queen mother of the west / Dwelling in a palace high in the Kunlun Mountains, the Queen Mother of the West, *Xī wáng mǔ*, is a fairy goddess from Taoist legend. She is known for her power to confer immortality, because she possesses two treasures, the pills of immortality and the peaches of immortality. The magic peaches grow only in her garden, and when they ripen, she holds the 'Banquet of the Peaches.' She is often depicted gracefully riding a crane or floating on clouds, attended by two young girls, Jade Maiden, *Yu nǔ*, who carries a fan, and Spirit Maiden, *Shén nǔ*, who carries the peaches of immortality. Her appearance has not always been beautiful and dignified. Originally the Queen Mother was part human and part animal, with tiger teeth, tangled hair, and a panther's tail. Over time she became more goddesslike. She is also the wife of the famous Great Jade Emperor, *Yù huáng dà dì*.

西王母 ■ 道教傳說中住在昆侖山的西王母，是仙界第一夫人，集生殺大權於一身。因為她擁有兩大法寶：天下獨一無二的長生不死藥和食之可與天地同壽的王母桃。這種仙桃只栽種在她的花園裡，當仙桃熟時，她就舉辦「蟠桃盛會」。她常被描寫成儀表雍容華貴，由捧著長壽仙桃的玉女和神女陪伴，悠雅地駕鶴雲游。但是，西王母的原始面貌，卻是虎牙、豹尾、披髮、狂嘯的半人半獸的部族圖騰。隨著時間的演化，她最終成為美麗的女仙之首，玉皇大帝的王母娘娘。

moon goddess / Chang E, known as the Moon Goddess, achieved eternal life by stealing the pill of immortality from her husband, Hou Yi, the Divine Archer. The Queen Mother of the West had rewarded him with the pill for his heroic deeds. When nine ravens had transmuted into suns, so that ten suns appeared in the sky, Hou Yi had shot down the nine suns with his bow and arrow, saving the earth from being scorched. The Queen Mother instructed Hou Yi to fast for a year before taking the pill, so he hid the treasure in his home. When he was away, his beautiful wife, Chang E, found the pill

女月神 ■ 眾所周知，女月神即是嫦娥，偷吃了不死靈藥，而獲得永恆的生命。她丈夫后羿是個神奇的射手，因為連射九日，拯救黎民有功，王母娘娘特賜予他一包不死靈藥，他將藥包藏在家裡。一天，后羿外出，嫦娥發現這包不死靈藥，就全部吃下。不料吃藥之後，她即刻身輕若雲，飄飄然向月宮飛去，后羿追也追不上。為此，西王母懲罰她，將她變作一隻蟾蜍。不死靈藥則變成一隻玉兔，與之相伴。從此，嫦娥孤獨地生活在月上廣寒宮中。不過，後來的傳說將嫦娥演變為美麗的女月神，而與月亮的清輝聯係在一起。每到農曆八月十五的中秋節，人們就會講述起女月神嫦娥的故事。

and swallowed it. She became extremely light and flew to the moon, with Hou Yi chasing her, to no avail. On reaching the moon, Chang E was punished and turned into a toad. The pill of immortality was transformed into a jade hare, which became her only companion. Filled with regret, Chang E lived a lonely life in the Winter Palace on the moon. In later legend, she became beautiful once more, associated with the radiance and splendor of the moon. She is remembered during the midautumn Moon Festival, on the fifteenth day of the eighth lunar month, when the moon is fullest.

女壽仙 ■ 麻姑是著名的女壽仙，民間藝術經常把她畫成駕鶴或騎鹿、捧著仙桃、酒或佛手，這些都象徵著長壽。雖然說她長得像個十八、九歲的美麗姑娘，可實際年齡卻無法計算。麻姑曾自云：「已見東海三為桑田」，而滄海變一次桑田，卻不知要化費多少千千萬萬年。在《西遊記》的故事中，麻姑前去赴王母娘娘的壽辰蟠桃會，特別獻上親自釀製的靈芝酒，作為祝壽之禮。因此廣為人知的《麻姑獻壽圖》就經常成為向女性壽星祝壽時的禮物之一，壽星翁的形象則用於男性壽星的壽辰。在清朝，「麻姑獻壽」的戲曲進入皇宮，為高官祝壽演出。

goddess of longevity / Ma Gu, the well-known Goddess of Longevity, is often depicted in folk art flying on a crane; riding a deer; or holding peaches, wine, or the fruit known as Buddha's hand, all symbols of long life. She has the forever-youthful appearance of an eighteen- or nineteen-year-old girl, though her actual age is infinite. Ma Gu has seen the Eastern Sea transform three times, each transformation said to take millions upon millions of years. In the classic novel 'Journey to the West,' *Xī yóu jì*, Ma Gu attended the peach banquet for the Queen Mother of the West's birthday, for which

she brewed a special wine made from the magic fungus, *líng zhī*. She gave this as a gift to the Queen Mother, and the image of this scene has since become renowned as 'Ma Gu offers longevity', *Má gū xiàn shòu*. It is given as a gift on an elder woman's birthday, while the image of the God of Longevity is the preferred image for celebrating the birthday of a man. During the Qing dynasty (1661–1911), a play was created depicting Ma Gu's story, *Má gū xiàn shòu*, and it became one of the plays performed in the imperial palace on a high official's birthday.

女壽仙的傳說

晉代的《神仙傳》（葛洪著）中，描寫女壽仙麻姑是個漂亮的姑娘，穿著文彩繡衣，擁有非凡的本領，一是能穿著木屐在水上行走，二是能擲米成丹砂，可見其精通煉丹術。她的哥哥，東海的王方平，精通天文圖讖，棄官入山修道，成了仙人。

據古籍《列仙全傳》（明‧王世貞著）記載，麻姑的父親麻秋，是北朝十六國以殘暴出名的將軍。他驅趕民伕服役，「築城嚴酷，晝夜不止，惟至雞鳴少息」。麻姑十分同情這些民伕，常常偷學雞叫，她一叫，群雞相效而啼，民伕就能早點收工。後來，她父親查出了她的所作所為，大發雷霆，到處搜捕她。麻姑潛逃入深山修道，終於成了女壽仙。

legends of the goddess of longevity / In 'The Classic of Immortals,' *Shén xiān zhuàn,* from the Jin dynasty (265–420), Ma Gu, the Goddess of Longevity, is described as a beautiful girl who wore exquisitely embroidered clothes and possessed unusual qualities. She was able to walk on water while wearing clogs and could turn rice into cinnabar, a sign that she had mastered alchemy. Her brother, Wang Fang Ping of the Eastern Sea, was a master of astrology who left his life as an official to seek the Taoist way and attain enlightenment in the mountains.

A text from the Ming dynasty (1368–1644), 'Complete Compendium of Immortals,' *Liè xiān quán zhuàn,* relates that Ma Gu's father was the infamously cruel and brutal general Ma Qiu of the Sixteen Kingdoms period (304–439). He enlisted laborers to build the city, and he forced them to work throughout the night. Only at the crack of dawn, when the roosters crowed, would he allow them to take a rest. Ma Gu sympathized with the laborers, so she secretly learned to imitate a rooster's call. When she crowed, the other roosters followed suit, allowing the laborers to get off work early. Learning of her deeds, her father was infuriated and went in search of her. Ma Gu stole away to the mountains and was transformed into the Goddess of Longevity.

八仙 ■ 道教傳說中的八仙，搜羅了社會生活各階層的代表人物，男女老幼、富貴貧賤、文莊粗野、貴族平民……每個人物都通過修道、奉獻和犧牲，造就了不朽的生命。八仙的故事，起初出現在唐宋時代，但大部份人物在元代才確定下來，八人組成一班。作為生命永恆的象徵，他們的形象被供奉在廟裡，受人崇拜。

eight immortals /
Legendary Taoist figures, the Eight Immortals embody various conditions of life and society, such as wealth and poverty, old age and youth, masculinity and femininity, and nobility and commoner. Each had been born human and attained immortality through an act of dedication, morality, or sacrifice. Individual stories of the Eight Immortals began to appear in the Tang and Song dynasties (618–1279), though they became a group only in the Yuan dynasty (1279–1368). Their images are worshiped in temples, and they are revered as a symbol of eternal life.

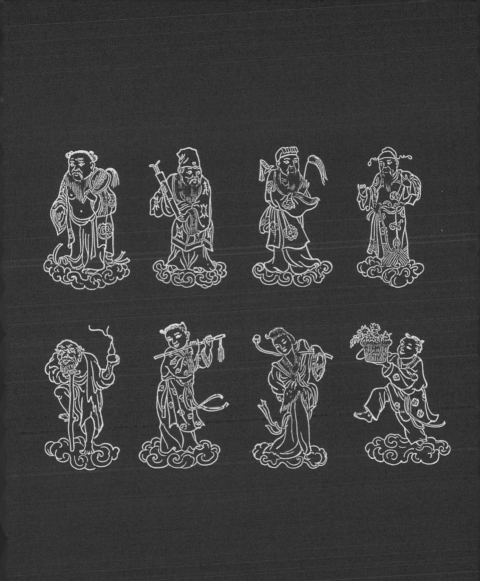

legend of the eight immortals / The renowned story 'The Eight Immortals Cross the Sea,' *Bā xiān guò hǎi,* recounts that they attended a banquet at the Jasper palace of the Queen Mother of the West. During the banquet the Eight Immortals (seven men and one woman) merrily drank until they were intoxicated. After saying farewell to the Queen Mother, they used their magic treasures to cross the Eastern Sea to go home. Li Tie Guai called upon his iron staff, Zhong Li Quan relied on a feathery fan, Zhang Guo Lao rode a paper donkey, Lu Dong Bin used a flute, Han Xiang Zi traveled on a flower basket, and He Xian Gu crossed on a bamboo umbrella. Lan Cai He and Cao Guo Jiu rode on jade boards. The Eastern Sea's Dragon King had two sons, Mo Jie and Long Du, and this showy display caught their eye. Consumed with greed, the brothers seized Lan Cai He and his treasure and dove deep into the ocean. The remaining Immortals went in pursuit and battled with the brothers, killing Mo Jie and injuring Long Du. In vengeance, the Dragon King enlisted the help of all the dragon kings in the sea to fight the Eight Immortals, but the kings were overwhelmingly defeated. Finally, the Buddhist deities Ru Lai and Guan Yin acted as mediators to resolve the hostilities. The Eight Immortals are much admired for their legendary teamwork and supernatural abilities.

八仙的傳說

著名的「八仙過海」故事說的是王母娘娘在瑤池設宴，款待八仙。八仙開懷暢飲，喝得酩酊大醉。辭謝王母之後，經東海取道回家。乘著興致，各自拿出法寶，渡越東海。李鐵拐立於鐵拐杖之上，乘風逐浪而渡。接著，鍾離權以拂塵、張果老用紙驢、呂洞賓以洞簫、韓湘子以花籃、何仙姑以竹罩、藍采和曹國舅用拍板、玉版，分別投水而渡。他們大顯神通，引起了東海龍王之子摩揭和龍毒的注意。兩兄弟見實起了貪心，搶了藍采和的拍板並將他擄入海中。另外七仙大怒，一場廝殺之後，斬了摩揭，傷了龍毒。為了復仇，四海龍王齊來參戰，但仍被有神力的八仙勢不可擋地擊敗。結果，經如來佛和觀音菩薩出面調解說項，大家最終消仇和解。八仙超自然的非凡本領和團隊精神，受到了人們高度的稱讚。

靈芝 ■ 靈芝,被認作為仙藥,其實是棗紅色的蕈類植物,中醫入藥,有滋補作用。靈芝作為吉祥物,被高度評價,主要在於寓意祝福,祈願健康長壽。古籍記載說,食靈芝者能起死回生,長生不老。按道教傳統說法,靈芝仙草生長在三仙山,那裡神仙集居。

在吉祥圖畫中,靈芝仙草經常被鹿或鶴啣在嘴裡,雙倍地表達長壽之意。它蘑菇狀或雲形頂部,正是創造如意的靈感來源。當靈芝和兩條鯰魚組合在一起,表示「年年如意」的寓意,因為「鯰」與「年」諧音。靈芝的形象,經常出現在中國傳統繪畫創作以及道教廟宇的壁畫中。

fungus of immortality /
Líng zhī, the fungus of immortality, is a burgundy-colored fungus (*Polyporus lucidus*) considered to have vital nutritive value in Chinese medicine. It is also a highly prized symbol of longevity. According to classical texts, it gives eternal life to those who consume it and has the super-natural ability to revive the dead. In Taoist tradition, the sacred fungus grew on the Three Islands of the Immortals, *Sān xiān shān*, in the East China Sea, where immortals lived and the elixir of immortality flowed from a jade fountain. Penglai is the most well known of the three islands.

The sacred fungus is often shown being held in the mouth of a deer or crane, themselves symbols of long life, creating a symbol of double longevity. The mushroom- or cloud-shaped head of the fungus is said to have inspired the design of the *rú yì* scepter, a symbol of luck. When the sacred fungus is shown in conjunction with two catfish, it forms the rebus 'may your wishes come true year after year,' *nián nián rú yì*, as the word for 'catfish,' *nián*, sounds the same as the word for 'year.' The *líng zhī* motif is often seen in Chinese art, in Taoist pictures, and on temple walls.

菊 chrysanthemum (*jú*)

菊 ■ 「菊」與「久」發音相近，被賦予「永久」的含意。菊花在晚秋直至深冬凌霜盛開，不怕嚴寒，從而成為長壽的象徵。「菊」的發音也與「九」相似，所以第九個月被認為是摘花的最好季節。把菊同九隻鵪鶉畫在一起，寓意「九世同居」。

chrysanthemum / The word for 'chrysanthemum,' *jú*, is pronounced similarly to the word *jiǔ*, meaning 'forever.' This flower blooms in late autumn and through the winter despite the bitter cold, making it an emblem of longevity. The word also sounds like 'nine,' *jiǔ*, and therefore is associated with the ninth month, said to be the best time to pick the flowers. A drawing of chrysanthemum and nine quails conveys the sentiment 'may nine generations live under one roof in peace,' *jiǔ shì tóng jū*.

 久 forever (*jiǔ*)

narcissus / The characters for narcissus, *shuǐ xiān*, literally mean 'water immortal.' An image combining narcissus flowers, stones, and bamboo, *zhù*, is a rebus for 'the immortals wish you a long life,' *qún xiān zhù shòu*, as bamboo stands for 'wish' and stones, *shòu shí*, symbolize longevity. The fragrant narcissus blooms during the New Year period and brings luck for the coming year.

水仙 ■ 水仙雅稱「凌波仙子」。一幅畫有水仙、壽石和竹子的圖案，其吉祥寓意是「仙祝長生」、或「群仙拱壽」。馨香清絕的水仙在中國新年期間開放，意味著為來年帶來好運。

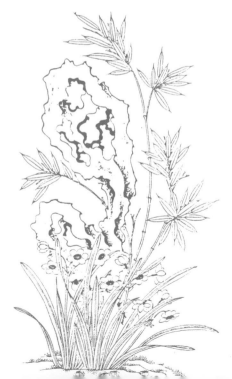

人參 ■ 價值很高的中國人參，被認為是長壽之源。人們相信這種根狀植物極有營養和具有療效，能治癒相當廣泛的慢性病，像感冒、頭痛、氣喘、高血壓和神經緊張。古人早就發現人參具有補氣，補充生命能量的藥效。它也被証明含有豐富礦物質，包括鐵、鈣、鉀、鋁和鎂。人參粗壯的根瘤極似人的手足，由此被稱為「人參」。根據不同的形狀、尺寸和效力，人參可以賣到相當高的價格。

ginseng / The Chinese highly value ginseng, *rén shēn*, as a potent source of longevity. This root is believed to possess nutritional and curative properties that can treat a wide range of ailments, such as colds, headaches, asthma, high blood pressure, and nervous disorders. The elderly regard it as a valuable medicine that can help build *qì*, vital energy. It has also been shown to contain many minerals, including iron, calcium, potassium, aluminum, and magnesium. Ginseng's sinewy protuberances resemble arms and legs, and *rén shēn* literally means 'man-shaped root.' Depending on potency, size, and shape, ginseng can fetch high prices.

長壽麵 ■ 長壽麵是一種手製細麵條，在老年人祝壽宴會上招待客人。在吃麵時，必須小心不要挾斷細長的麵條，否則會折壽，這一習俗至今仍很流行。據書載，唐玄宗之妻在生活困苦之時，曾脫下自己身上的紫色半臂衫，去換取長壽麵，給她丈夫過生日。

longevity noodles / Long wheat or rice noodles, known as 'longevity noodles,' are served at an elder's birthday dinner to symbolize the wish for a long life. During the Tang dynasty (618–907), the wife of Emperor Xuan Zong, during a period of hardship, exchanged a purple-colored shawl for longevity noodles to give her husband for his birthday. One should take care never to break the long noodles while eating them, as this would cut a life short.

longevity lock / Not until after one month of life, *mǎn yuè*, was a child's birth celebrated in ancient China, due to the high mortality rate. At this celebration, infants traditionally were given a longevity lock, a type of necklace that brought protection, health, and longevity. Often engraved with auspicious phrases, such as 'may you live to one hundred years,' *cháng mìng bǎi suì*, the lock is made from silver, gold, or copper, depending on the wealth of the household.

The longevity lock was origi- nally a five-colored rope orna- ment made of red, yellow, blue, white, and black strands and was hung outside the door to guard against evil. These colors

長命鎖　■　在古代中國，鑒於小孩的死亡率很高，人們在小孩滿月時就為其慶生日。給嬰兒送長命鎖（一種項鍊）作為禮物。這個傳統表達保祐、健康和長命之祝願，祝願孩子在未來，能適應不同的生活條件。

根據家人的富裕程度，鎖分別用金、銀或銅製成。長命鎖由「長命索」演化而來。長命索通常以紅、黃、藍、白、黑五色絲線編織而成，五色分別代表東、西、南、北、中五方，被認為具有神力，懸掛在門外，可以避邪除瘟，保障兒童健康。後來，五色線演變為「長命縷」或「百索」，掛在小孩的脖子上，以求保祐。在舊時北平，新生孩子的家庭會請人挨家挨戶去乞討銅錢，然後集在一起，為嬰兒打製成長命鎖，稱為「化百家鎖」。這鎖代表著來自一百家的祝福和保祐。

represent the five directions—north, south, east, west, and center—which were believed to have protective powers. In later tradition, a five-colored string was hung around a child's neck for protection and became known as 'longevity thread,' *cháng mìng lǔ*, or 'one hundred rope,' *bǎi suǒ*. In Beiping (now Beijing), families with newborns sent someone out to beg for copper coins from many households. A longevity lock was then made for the infant from the coins. This was called the 'one hundred lives lock,' *huà bǎi jiā suǒ*, and represented the blessings and protection of one hundred households.

nine *(jiǔ)*

nine / The number nine is an extremely propitious number as it is a pun on the word 'forever,' *jiǔ*. At New Year, the first meal often consists of nine dishes or courses. Many emperors gave the number nine great importance: the total sum of buildings in the imperial palace often added up to a multiple of nine, and in the Ming and Qing dynasties (1368–1911), the imperial palace was built with nine thousand nine hundred ninety-nine rooms. Objects were given names with the word 'nine': 'nine-dragon wall,' 'nine-dragon cup.' The number also has mysterious properties: when nine is multiplied by any other number, the sum of the digits of the resulting figure, when added together, always equals nine (6 x 9 = 54; 5 + 4 = 9).

久

= forever (*jiǔ*)

「九」字

「九」、「久」同音，所以成為特別吉祥的數字。新年的第一餐，往往由九盤菜或九道菜組成。許多皇帝都高度重視「九」字的意義，例如，皇宮裡宮殿的總數通常是九的倍數。在明清時期，皇宮有九千九百九十九個房間。物體也用「九」字相稱：九龍壁或九龍杯。中國人還發現了「九」字神秘的性質，比如，當「九」字與任何其它數字相乘，其答數的個別數字之和，必定是「九」字。（六乘九等於五十四，五加四等於九）。

double happiness

Double happiness is synonymous with one of life's most important celebrations—marriage. Consequently, it is related to the wish for fertility, and is often seen at wedding banquets. The good luck that surrounds this character has made it ubiquitous, and it commonly appears on bowls, glasses, vases, product packaging, and other everyday objects. The character for double happiness is traditionally displayed as a cutout or inscription on red paper, red being a lucky color. The desire for marital bliss is expressed in numerous proverbial sayings, such as 'may you grow old together in harmony,' *bái tóu xié lăo*, and 'may you be blessed with one hundred sons and one thousand grandsons,' *băi zĭ qiān sūn*. The mandarin duck, the magpie, the lotus, the pomegranate, and the Gods of Peace and Harmony are symbols for marriage and fertility.

「雙喜」與人生最重要的慶典——婚禮相聯，因為這關係到對生育的祈望。在婚禮宴會上，通常都可以看到這個「雙喜」的圖符。由於「雙喜」包含極為吉祥的意義，這個圖符在日常生活中應用極廣，例如盤子、玻璃杯、花瓶、產品包裝以及日用品等。在傳統上，「雙喜」圖符均以紅紙剪成，或書寫在紅紙上，因為紅色被視作吉祥之色。不少成語，如「白頭偕老」、「百子千孫」等，都反映了對婚姻幸福的向往。鴛鴦、喜鵲、荷蓮、石榴以及和合二仙，都是明顯地象徵婚姻和生育的圖案。

「雙喜」字 ■ 從古至今，在慶賀新婚時，人們經常將剪紙或印製的「雙喜」字，貼在牆上、門上、窗上。新房裡都被裝飾著大紅「雙喜」字。此外，紅色是吉祥喜慶之色，可引來好運，所以新娘子總要穿紅色禮服。這個風俗的起源，可以追溯到宋朝。

double happiness character / Paper cutouts or prints of the double happiness character, *xǐ*, are often pasted on walls, doors, and windows when a wedding celebration takes place. Traditionally, the bridal chamber was decorated with large red *xǐ* characters. In addition to attracting luck, red is the color of joy and happiness, and thus the bride always wears red. The origins of this practice can be traced back to the Song dynasty (960–1279).

「雙喜」字的傳說

宋代宰相王安石二十三歲那年，赴京趕考，住在汴梁（開封）舅父家。一天，經過東京富貴大族馬員外家時，看見門外熙熙攘攘，擠滿觀眾。原來馬員外在門口貼出了一副上聯：「走馬燈，燈馬走，燈熄馬停步。」誰能對出下聯，誰就能娶他才貌雙全的女兒為妻。王安石自負才學過人，脫口而出：「好對呀好對！」馬府的老管家聽到了，馬上過來請他去見馬員外，因為這上聯已經貼出六個月了，至今尚無人對出。由於王安石一時還未想好下聯，明日要去赴考，今日更無時間思考答對，便不辭而別。

第二天，王安石在考場上，見試題不難，就文思大發，一揮而就。主考大人見他年紀輕輕、才華出眾，就傳他面試，指著廳前的飛虎旗說：「飛虎旗，旗虎飛，旗卷虎藏身。」命王安石立即答對。王安石猛想起昨日在馬家門外看到的上聯，正好作對，便不加思索地答道：「走馬燈，燈馬走，燈熄馬停步。」主考大人對他的才思敏捷，對答如流，印象格外深刻。

legend of the double happiness character / During the Song dynasty (960–1279), a young and talented man who would later become prime minister, Wang An Shi, went to the capital, Bianliang (today's Kaifeng), to sit for the imperial exam. On arriving, he passed a crowd of people gathered around the residence of the wealthy Ma family. Ma was offering his daughter's hand in marriage to anyone who could compose the second half of the incomplete 'couplet,' *duì lián,* that he had posted outside his house. This Chinese pastime of testing high literary skill required that the second line match the first in character count, syntax, structure, and artistic merit. Wang found this a particularly fine couplet and the challenge appealing. Seeing Wang's enthusiasm, Ma's servant asked him to meet Ma, since no one had been able to match the couplet for over six months. Wang, however, could not linger because he had to take the exam the next day.

The exam proved less difficult than Wang had anticipated. The examiner, seeing that Wang was extraordinarily sharp and brilliant, indicated he would like to meet him in person. Wishing to test Wang's quick-wittedness, he presented him with an incomplete couplet to finish on the spot. Coincidentally, the structure of the couplet's first line was identical to the one hanging outside Ma's house. Wang recognized this relationship and recited the line from Ma's couplet effortlessly to complete this couplet. The examiner was highly impressed.

After the exam, Wang passed Ma's house, and this time, when invited to reply to the challenge, he recited the half-couplet the examiner had just given him. Wang was granted the hand of

考試完畢，王安石在返回舅舅家時，途經馬員外家門，等候多時的老管家一眼認出，連忙邀請他去見馬員外，對完下聯。王安石揮筆寫出：「飛虎旗，旗虎飛，旗卷虎藏身。」字體遒勁，對答工整，頓時贏得了馬小姐的含羞應承。

第三天行婚禮時，兩個報子高聲來報，王安石已中頭名狀元，成就了最顯赫的功名業績。王安石金榜題名恰遇洞房花燭，喜上加喜，「雙喜臨門」。他喜氣洋洋地大筆一揮，在紅紙上寫了斗大的「雙喜」字。從此，兩個喜字不再分開，成為婚禮的吉祥圖符。

Ma's daughter in marriage, and the wedding ceremony was held the following day. At the same time, news arrived that Wang had passed the imperial exam and attained the top position, *zhuàng yuan,* an extremely distinguished accomplishment.

These two happinesses had arrived simultaneously, *shuāng xǐ lín mén,* inspiring Wang to pick up a brush and write two large 'happiness,' or *xǐ,* characters on red paper. From that moment on, the double happiness symbol became inseparably linked to matrimony.

god of double happiness / Among the gods, the God of Double Happiness is one of the most difficult to visualize because he has no physical form and his presence can only be felt. In ancient times the God of Double Happiness, *xǐ shén*, brought a lifetime of happiness and good fortune and was integral to a wedding ceremony. Feng shui masters were called on the wedding day to determine the direction in which the God of Double Happiness might be found that day. Once the direction was determined, the bride entered the ceremonial sedan chair and its entrance was turned to face his direction. The bride took a moment to 'beckon the God of Double Happiness,' *yíng xǐ shén*, before setting off for the ceremony. In the Qing dynasty (1661–1911), feng shui masters created a book to aid in locating his direction, which changed day to day.

喜神 ■ 在所有的神靈之中，喜神是最抽象的一位，因為它的形象是那麼不可捉摸，但又必須能夠被感覺到。對於古代婚禮來說，喜神絕對是不可缺少的，他能給一生帶來喜慶吉祥。舉行婚禮的那天，往往要請風水先生來測定喜神所在的方向，因為這個方向位置每天每時變幻無定。一旦經風水先生確定，新娘上轎以後，轎口必須對準喜神所在的方向，稍停片刻，以招呼喜神，叫做「迎喜神」，然後再出發去進行婚禮儀式。到了清朝，風水先生終於撰著了辨別喜神方向的書。

喜神 ■ 也有說喜神的傳統源於舊時北平的妓院。在新年來臨之際，一般百姓帶著食物果品走親訪友，但是由於妓女的社會地位很低，串門拜年沒有她們的份。為生計，她們還要拉住富裕的顧客，於是她們便拉上相好的去「走喜神方」，也即順著雞叫的方向，去碰喜神。她們相信「遇得喜神，則能致一歲康寧」，大發其財。

god of double happiness /
The origin of the God of Double Happiness is also said to come from the brothels of old Beijing (known then as Beiping). Because prostitutes occupied a low social position, they did not participate in New Year's visits, a custom of bringing food and fruit as gifts to friends and relatives on the second day of the New Year celebration. Instead, they were escorted by one of their wealthy patrons to seek the God of Double Happiness, who was believed to be found in the direction from which the roosters crowed. The prostitutes believed that if they came upon this god, their lives would be blessed with good fortune and health in the upcoming year.

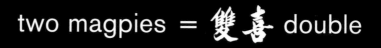

two magpies = 雙喜 double

happiness (*shuāng xǐ*)

喜鵲 ■ 人們稱喜鵲為「報喜之鳥」，先秦時代，人們認為喜鵲具有感應預兆之特異本領，可以預示客人、喜事或好運的到來。

一隻喜鵲棲息在梅枝上，傳遞「喜上眉梢」的祝願，因為「梅」與「眉」同音。兩隻喜鵲面對面的圖案，寓意「雙喜」、「喜相逢」，象徵婚姻美滿幸福。

傳說喜鵲還扮演著另一種角色，當夫妻分別時，他們要打破一面鏡子，分為兩半，一人各持一半。如果妻子在家和人私通，她那半邊的鏡子就會變成一隻喜鵲，飛到她丈夫那兒去。因此，人們常常以喜鵲圖案裝飾鏡子的背面。

magpie / The characters for 'magpie,' *xǐ que*, literally mean the 'bird of happiness.' A picture of two magpies facing each other stands for 'double happiness,' *shuāng xǐ*, symbolic of conjugal bliss. The call of a magpie foretells the arrival of a guest, good news, or good fortune. A magpie resting on a plum branch conveys the wish 'happiness before one's brow,' *xǐ shàng méi shāo*, as the word for 'plum' and 'brow' are both pronounced *méi*. Magpies also served to preserve the integrity of a marriage, according to legend. When a husband and wife were to be apart for any reason, they would break a mirror and each take half. If the wife was unfaithful, her half of the mirror turned into a magpie that flew back and informed her husband. Consequently, an image of a magpie is often placed on the back of a mirror.

喜鵲的傳說

相傳，玉皇大帝的孫女——織女，住在天河之東，年復一年辛勤地織著雲錦天衣。天帝憐憫她生活孤單，就允許她嫁給河之西的牛郎。但她有了美滿的婚姻，卻疏忽了自己的職責，這就觸怒了天帝。天帝將她遣回河之東，以示懲罰，並只允許她一年一度，與她丈夫在天河上相會。在七月初七那天，喜鵲在天河上架起了「鵲橋」，牛郎織女終於得以團聚。這就是家喻戶曉的「鵲橋相會」的故事。

牛郎織女

legend of the magpie / According to a well-known lovers' tale, there lived a weaver who was the granddaughter of the Heavenly Jade Emperor, *Yù huáng dà dì*. She lived alone on the east side of the river, laboring year after year at weaving beautiful silk robes. The emperor felt sympathy for her solitary life and gave her permission to marry the cowherd across the river. Once they were married, however, she neglected her weaving duties, which angered the emperor. To punish her, he sent her back to the other side of the river, and decreed that she be allowed to reunite with her husband only once a year, on the seventh night of the seventh month. It is said that a flock of magpies form a bridge allowing the lovers to meet.

鴛鴦 ■ 古人稱鴛鴦為匹鳥，其同飛共戲，相伴不離，因此被認為是夫妻和諧幸福的象徵。一對鴛鴦和蓮花在一起即構成《鴛鴦貴子》圖案，由於「蓮」與「連」諧音，所以寓意祝願新婚夫妻連連生子。吉祥語「鴛鴦福祿」中，一對鴛鴦代表對新娘與新郎幸福美滿生活的祝福。以鴛鴦為題材的吉祥圖案，在漢代即已出現，流傳至今仍廣泛應用於結婚禮品如枕頭、床單或手帕上。

mandarin ducks / Because they live in pairs and mate for life, mandarin ducks, *yuān yang*, are a symbol of marital happiness and harmony. A pair of mandarin ducks accompanied by a lotus flower represents a long, harmonious marriage blessed with many children because lotus, *lián*, sounds identical to 'continuous.' In the proverb *yuān yang fú lù*, a pair of mandarin ducks symbolizes 'may the bride and groom be blessed with luck and prosperity.' The ducks first appeared in drawings during the Han dynasty (206 B.C.–A.D. 220) and are still a common motif used on pillowcases, bedcovers, handkerchiefs, and other wedding gifts to signify a happy couple.

鴛鴦的傳說

據傳，二千多年前，晉國大夫洪輔告老還鄉，大興土木，開闢林苑。他從外地請來了年輕的花匠怨哥，為其種花植草。次年清明節，怨哥正在為羅漢松培土，忽聽到蓮池裡有人驚呼「救命」，便奮不顧身躍入蓮池，救起了洪府千金映妹。洪輔見此情景，以為怨哥調戲女兒，遂將其痛打並下入大牢。入夜，映妹來探怨哥，帶來五彩寶衣給他穿上。洪輔聽說後，更加惱怒成羞，剝下怨哥的衣服，縛石將其推下蓮池。映妹得知此事，痛不欲生，亦躍身入池。第二天清晨，人們看到蓮池中出現了兩隻奇異的鳥兒，雄的五彩繽紛，雌的毛色蒼褐，雙飛雙宿，恩愛無比，人人都說這是怨哥和映妹的精靈所化。

legend of mandarin ducks / Two thousand years ago, when China consisted of many small countries, a senior official by the name of Hong Fu from Jin Country retired and returned to his hometown. As he enjoyed building, Hong Fu decided to establish a park, and he invited a young gardener, Yuan Ge, to cultivate the garden. The following spring while planting trees during Qing Ming festival, the day of remembrance for the dead, Yuan Ge heard a cry for help coming from the park's lotus pond. Hong Fu's daughter Yang Mei had fallen into the water. Without hesitation the young man leapt in to save her. Instead of expressing gratitude, however, Hong Fu accused Yuan Ge of assaulting his daughter and threw him in prison. During the night, Yang Mei paid a visit to her rescuer and brought him an expensive coat with many beautiful colors. When Hong Fu heard this, he was livid and ripped the coat from Yuan Ge. He then tied the young man to a large stone and threw him into the lotus pond. When Yang Mei learned of this, she was so distraught she threw herself into the same pond. The next day, people saw a pair of strange birds in the lotus pond, the male wearing a vibrantly colored coat and the female an exquisitely beautiful one. They flew away together and were said to be the souls of Yuan Ge and Yang Mei.

鳳凰 ■ 鳳凰是神話裡虛構的神鳥，稱為「百鳥之王」，與龍、麒麟、龜等瑞獸靈禽一起並稱「四靈」。鳳凰經常和龍相配，以象徵喜慶和諧的結合。鳳凰的形象在結婚禮品中，代表女性，而龍代表男性。據說，鳳凰只有在君道清明的太平盛世才會出現。孔夫子曾悲嘆在他的時代，由於各國宮廷的腐敗漫延，鳳凰沒有出現。

在皇宮中，鳳凰和龍的圖案代表皇帝和皇后，而且歷來皇家的事物多冠以「鳳」字，例如，鳳輦、龍座。隨著時代的發展，民間也逐漸採用，並與婚姻的美滿幸福聯係起來。

phoenix / The mythical phoenix, *fèng huáng*, is the king of all birds and is one of the four supernatural creatures, along with the dragon, unicorn, and tortoise. The phoenix is often paired with the dragon to symbolize a happy and harmonious union. The phoenix represents the female essence, *fèng*, and the dragon represents the male, *huáng*, making this combination popular on wedding gifts. The bird is said to appear only in times of prosperity and peace, when the country is under sound rule. Confucius lamented that the phoenix was not to be seen in his time, as corruption was rife in the imperial courts.

The phoenix-and-dragon motif appeared on many articles of the imperial palace and came to represent the empress and emperor. The words 'phoenix' and 'dragon' commonly preceded the word for an object associated with the empress and emperor; the empress's sedan chair was termed 'phoenix carriage,' *feng niǎn*, and the emperor's throne was known as the 'dragon seat,' *lóng zuò*. Gradually, the motif was adopted by the common people and came to be associated with marital bliss.

legend of the phoenix / During the Spring Autumn and Warring States periods (770–221 B.C.), there was a man named Xiao Shi who was highly adept at playing the flute. He was so skilled that he could attract peacocks, white cranes, and other birds to the courtyard garden. Nong Yu, the daughter of Duke Qin Mu Gong, fell in love with Xiao Shi, and her father consented to their marriage. Once married, Xiao Shi taught Nong Yu to play the flute and to imitate the cry of the phoenix. After a few years, Nong Yu had mastered the phoenix's call. One day a phoenix suddenly flew down from the sky and landed on the roof of their house. The two climbed onto the bird's back and it flew off into the sky. Since then, pictures of flute players enchanting the phoenix have symbolized marital harmony.

鳳凰的傳說

在春秋戰國的秦穆公時代，有一個名叫蕭史的人，精通吹簫。他精妙的簫聲能把孔雀、白鶴等禽鳥召引到庭院中來。秦穆公的女兒弄玉愛上了蕭史，而且秦穆公也同意了他們的婚事。婚後，蕭史教弄玉用簫模擬鳳凰鳴叫的聲音。幾年之後，弄玉模擬鳳鳴維妙維肖。一天，一隻鳳凰從空中飛下來，棲息在他們的屋頂上，於是他們同駕鳳凰而去。從此，「吹簫引鳳」就成為美滿婚姻的象徵。

麒麟 ■ 作為中國古人想象中的「仁獸」、「靈獸」，麒麟常被描繪成麋身、牛尾、魚鱗、五趾蹄和頭上有一角。其雄者曰麒，雌者曰麟。麒麟的形象首先出現在秦朝秦始皇帝的宮苑中。民間吉祥圖案畫一童子持蓮抱笙，乘麒麟從天而降，「蓮」和「笙」，與「連生」諧音，寓意「麒麟送子」「連生貴子」。

qí lín / An auspicious mythical creature known in legend since ancient times, the *qí lín* has most commonly been described as having a deer's torso, an ox's tail, fish scales, five-toed feet, and a horn on its head. *Qí* represents the male, and *lín* the female. The *qí lín* was first seen on the imperial palace grounds of Emperor Qin Shi Huangdi in the Qin dynasty (221–206 B.C.).

In folk art, a popular image depicts a small child riding on the back of a *qí lín*, signifying '*qí lín* delivers children,' *qí lín sòng zǐ*. In one hand, the child holds a lotus flower, a symbol of continuity, expressing the wish for the 'continual birth of children.'

鯉魚 ■ 描繪一對鯉魚的圖案，象徵和諧相愛，成為極好的結婚禮物。由於鯉魚產子多，常被用作祈求多子多孫的吉祥象徵。成語「如魚得水」，用來描寫新婚夫妻和諧幸福的生活。

carp / A pair of carp symbolizes love and harmony, and is a frequent motif on wedding gifts. Because the carp produces many eggs, it is seen as an auspicious symbol for an abundance of children. The phrase 'fish in water,' *rú yú dé shuǐ*, means being in one's natural state and is a metaphor for a harmonious marriage. This phrase is often symbolized by an image of two fish.

蜘蛛 ■ 蜘蛛又稱「蟢子」，「蟢」與「喜」同音，因此在古代被聯想為預報喜兆的小昆蟲。畫一隻蜘蛛從蛛網中心，沿著蛛絲往下垂，寓意「喜從天降」。蛛網因其形狀，而比擬外圓內方的古錢，「錢眼」與「眼前」諧音，所以畫蜘蛛和古錢在一起，則寓意「喜在眼前」。

spider / Considered a good omen for happiness, the spider, *xǐ zi*, sounds identical to 'happiness,' *xǐ*. It has come to be known as the 'happy insect,' and a picture of a spider dropping from the center of its web is a rebus for 'happiness dropping from the sky,' *xǐ cóng tiān jiàng*. The web resembles ancient money, because it is round on the outside and square on the inside. The square hole in the web is considered an eye and therefore expresses 'happiness before one's eyes,' *xǐ zài yǎn qián*.

蟢子 spider (*xǐ zi*)

喜 happiness (*xǐ*)

爆竹 ■ 放爆竹是一種驅魔祛邪，祈望來年平安好運的傳統，幾乎與農曆新年成了同義詞。放爆竹也應用於其它慶典，如婚禮、開張營業等，以增加歡樂和喜氣，但沒有了迷信的意義。如今，大城市裡已禁止燃放爆竹，改用錄有爆竹聲的錄音帶替代。

自唐代起，有人將火藥裝進竹筒裡，點燃後能發出巨響，稱之為「爆竹」，以驅鬼保平安。畫一個兒童點燃爆竹的圖案，正是表達「竹報平安」的吉祥意義。到了宋代，人們用紙製的筒子代替竹子，把爆竹編成串，稱為「編炮」或「鞭炮」。爆竹全用紅紙包裹，因為傳說中的怪獸「年」害怕紅色，新年期間，人們穿紅色衣服，掛紅色燈籠與放爆竹，都出於同一原因。

firecrackers / Traditionally set off to guard against evil spirits and ensure peace and fortune for the upcoming year, firecrackers are synonymous with New Year. They are also ignited for many other celebrations, including weddings or the opening of a business, more to add a festive and auspicious atmosphere, *xǐ qìng*, than to frighten away evil spirits. Today an audio recording of exploding firecrackers is used in large cities where fireworks are prohibited.

During the Tang dynasty (618–907), gunpowder was placed inside bamboo stems to create *bào zhú*, or 'exploding bamboo.' The common phrase *zhú bào píng ān*, 'wishing you peace,' is symbolized by a boy lighting a firecracker because bamboo is pronounced the same as 'to wish.' In the Song dynasty (960–1279), people began manufacturing firecrackers using paper tubes instead of bamboo, attaching them together to form *biān pào*, a string of firecrackers. They are always red to scare off the beast *Nián*, who fears that color. Throughout the New Year celebration, people wear red clothes and hang red lanterns, as well as set off firecrackers.

爆竹的傳說

相傳在太古時代，在深山老林裡有一種殘忍的怪獸，叫「年」，每當寒冬將盡，新春快來之際，就要出來找人吃。人們與「年」鬥過幾次之後，發現「年」害怕響聲、光和紅色，便在年末歲首，將竹子放進火裡燒熱爆裂，發出極大的響聲，把怪獸趕走。這樣，原始的爆竹便發明出來了。

legend of firecrackers / A ferocious mythical monster, *Nián*, whose name means 'year,' once terrorized the common people. He lived in the remote mountains and emerged once every New Year's Eve to prey on humans. The people battling the monster at last realized he was afraid of noise, light, and the color red. They also discovered that bamboo placed in the fire would pop and crack loudly, as heat caused the air inside the jointed stems to expand, shattering the bamboo with an explosive sound and scaring away the beast. Thus the first firecrackers were invented.

gods of unity and harmony /

Hé hé èr xiān are the Gods of Unity and Harmony, who represent marriage, love, and reunification. In portrayals of the two laughing gods, Han Shan holds a round box, *hé*, and Shi De carries a lotus, also pronounced *hé*. Respectively, they form rebuses for 'unity,' *hé hǎo*, and 'harmony,' *hé xié*. Their pictures were often hung at wedding ceremonies to symbolize the harmonious union of two people, *hé xié hǎo hé*. This tradition is now less frequent, but their images still remain popular.

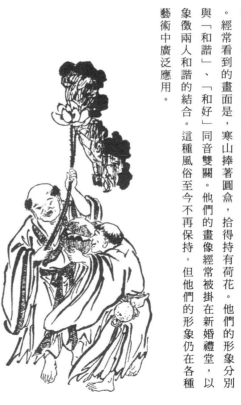

和合二仙 ■ 和合二仙是兩位笑口常開的神仙，代表婚姻、愛情和復合。經常看到的畫面是，寒山捧著圓盒，拾得持有荷花。他們的形象分別與「和諧」、「和好」同音雙關。他們的畫像經常被掛在新婚禮堂，以象徵兩人和諧的結合。這種風俗至今不再保持，但他們的形象仍在各種藝術中廣泛應用。

和合神的傳說

和合二仙源於唐代的寒山和拾得和尚。他們同住一村，是親如兄弟的知己朋友，同愛一女，但互不相知。拾得臨婚時，寒山始知，便棄家到蘇州楓橋，削髮為僧。拾得知情後，亦舍女來江南尋寒山。探得其住處後，乃折一枝盛開的荷花前往禮之，寒山一見，即手捧一盒齋飯出迎。二人相見樂極，相向而舞。遂同為僧人，開山立廟，建「寒山寺」。

另一位和合神源於唐代鐃州（今屬河南）的萬回。他「生而痴愚，至八九歲方能語」。他的兄長在遼東服役多年，久絕音信，有傳聞說其已死，其父母心痛欲絕。萬回安慰他們，並保証去找尋兄長。次日一早，萬回離家，「出門如飛，馬馳不及，及暮而還」，稟告父母曰：「兄平安無事。」並帶來兄長之親筆信，「緘封猶濕」。鑒於他往返一日，即行萬里，可見其非一般凡人，而具有神力，故號稱「萬回」。由於他使家人團聚，在宋代被尊崇為「和合之神」。有時也被稱為萬回哥哥，到了明清時期，則漸變為和合二仙了。

legends of the gods of unity and harmony / The Gods of Unity and Harmony originated in the Tang dynasty (618–907) as the monks Han Shan and Shi De. They lived in a small village in the north of China and were friends as intimate as devoted brothers. As youths, they both fell in love with the same girl. Just before Shi De was to marry her, Han Shan learned of the upcoming wedding and immediately departed for Suzhou to become a monk. On hearing this, Shi De gave up the girl and went looking for Han Shan to bring him a blossoming lotus flower. Han Shan was overjoyed at seeing him and presented Shi De with a round box containing a vegetarian meal. They danced with joy at being reunited. Shi De stayed to became a monk as well, and together the two friends established a temple called the Temple of Han Shan.

◇◇◇

Another account tells of a monk named Wan Hui, from Wenzhou (now Henan province), born early in the Tang dynasty (618–907). He was born a simpleton and unable to speak until the age of eight or nine. For many years, his parents had not received news from his brother, who was serving in the army in distant Liaodong, and they were distraught when one day they heard that he might have been killed. The boy consoled his parents, promising to go in search of his brother, and set out early the next day. He returned by evening to report that his brother was alive and well, and brought back a letter confirming his well-being. This feat indicated that he was not an ordinary person but possessed supernatural abilities, and he was subsequently named Wan Hui, meaning 'returning from ten thousand *lǐ*' (over three thousand miles). Since he had reunited his family, he was given the title God of Unity and Harmony. Sometimes known as Brother Wan Hui, *Wàn huí gē ge,* he subsequently became two gods during the late Ming and early Qing dynasties.

蓮　■　由於蓮蓬多籽，並與花同時生長，「蓮」與「連」同音雙關，蓮籽與「連子」諧音，故蓮借寓「連生貴子」之意。蓮花有並蒂同心者，為一蒂兩花，這是男女好合與夫妻恩愛的象徵。蓮與任何祝詞相配，都具有祝福連續不斷之意，例如好運、富足、高升或生子。蓮花也稱荷花，「荷」與「和」、「合」諧音，所以一張畫著兩朵蓮花的圖案，象徵「和睦相愛」。藕斷絲連，也寓「連」之意。

蓮花在佛教上被尊崇為西方淨土的聖潔象徵，佛身多置於蓮花座上。據說佛教創始人釋迦牟尼在他的家鄉盛植蓮花，色有青、黃、紅、白等多種。

lotus / Because the lotus can blossom and bear fruit simultaneously, it is fitting that one word for 'lotus,' *lián*, is pronounced the same as the words 'to repeat' and 'continuous.' Lotus seeds, *lián zǐ*, express a potent message for the 'continual birth of children,' because *zǐ* means both 'seed' and 'child.' Two lotus flowers blooming from the same base or stem symbolize harmony between a husband and wife. Coupled with various other images, the lotus can represent the wish for the continuity

of luck, wealth, promotion, or children. The lotus root, *lián ǒu*, consisting of long strands that refuse to break, is a metaphor for 'continuity,' *lián*. Another word for 'lotus,' *hé huā*, makes a play on the words 'harmony' and 'together-ness,' both pronounced *hé*. A picture of two lotus flowers therefore represents 'harmony and love,' *hé mù xiāng ài*.

The Buddha is often seen seated on a lotus flower, which is also a sacred emblem of Buddhism, symbolizing purity. Lotus flowers of all colors were said to have grown in the birthplace of Siddhartha, the founder of Buddhism.

date / In China, being blessed with many offspring is regarded as one of life's great happinesses. *Zǎo*, the word for 'date,' has the same pronunciation as the word for 'early,' *zǎo*; thus the fruit embodies the meaning 'may you have children soon,' *zǎo shēng zǐ*. In the countryside of northern China, many courtyards are planted with date palms. The fruit serves not only as a source of food but also as a good omen for wealth: *zǎo fā cái*, 'may you become wealthy soon.' Dates are also thought to whet the appetite and to benefit the *qì*, or energy, of the body.

A picture of a date paired with a longan fruit, *guì yuán*, conveys the wish 'may you be blessed with many noble children soon,' *zǎo shēng guì zi*, as 'longan' is a pun on the word for noble, *guì*. When combined with a camphor tree, it expresses the wish to rise quickly to high office.

棗 ■ 在古代中國，多子多孫是人生最大的祈願。棗與「早」諧音，所以北方農村庭院多栽棗樹，除食用外，也為討個「早」的口彩，祈願「早發財」或「早生子」。棗也有較多的藥用價值，能開胃健脾，補中益氣。棗與桂圓組合的圖案，寓意「早生貴子」。棗樹與樟樹畫在一起，則表示祝願早生子獲高官。

栗 ■ 栗子，與「立子」同音，所以被作為早生求子的吉祥象徵。將栗子、荔枝和棗組合在一起的圖畫，表示祝願「早立子」。「栗」也與「禮」諧音，所以栗子被用以表示婦人贊。

在漢代就出現了將栗子和紅棗撒在新房裡，以祈願夫妻恩愛、多子多孫的風俗。到了唐朝，人們開始用古錢替代，以增加祝願富貴的含意。

chestnut / The word for chestnut, *lì zi*, contains the word 'to establish,' *lì*, so the chestnut is auspicious for those wishing to create a family. *Zǐ*, or seed, also means 'son' or 'child.' A picture of chestnuts, lichees, and dates together signifies 'may you establish children soon,' *zǎo lì zi*, because the date is a rebus for 'early,' *zǎo*, and the word for 'lichee,' *lì zi*, sounds the same as the word for 'chestnut.' The first sound in 'chestnut,' *lì*, is also identical to the word for 'courteous' or 'etiquette,' *lì*, and thus the chestnut has come to symbolize these desirable qualities in women.

In the Han dynasty (206 B.C.–A.D. 220), it was a custom to scatter dates and chestnuts in the bridal chamber as a way to wish that the happy couple have many children. By the Tang dynasty (618–907), people began using money instead, which embodied the additional meaning of the wish for wealth or prosperity.

花生 ■ 花生與「生」諧音，被認為是生育的象徵。在婚禮上，經常用一大盤花生來招待客人，一是表示「生」，二是表示「花著生」，既生男孩，又生女孩，兒女雙全。

peanut / *Huā shēng*, the peanut, is a symbol of fertility because *shēng* means 'to give birth,' and *huā* signifies many sons and daughters by allusion to *huā sè*, 'a great variety.' A bowl of peanuts is often present at a wedding to indicate good wishes for many sons and daughters.

melons and seeds /

Because they contain many seeds, melons are symbols of fertility. They also represent the wish for 'generation after generation of children and grandchildren,' *zǐ sūn wàn dài*, since long continuous vines connect fruits of varying sizes. Additionally, melon, *guā*, rhymes with the word for 'baby' or 'child,' *wá*. Pumpkin, *nán guā*, contains the word 'melon' and alludes to a male child because *nán* means 'male.' The birth of a son was highly desired and celebrated in ancient China and is often treated the same way today.

Melon seeds are sometimes seen at weddings to wish the couple the blessing of many children. Red seeds, the color of luck, invoke additional happiness.

瓜類與瓜籽 ■ 長藤蔓繞的瓜類合有眾多的種子，「瓜」與「娃」同韻，所以西瓜、南瓜，冬瓜、西葫蘆等都被認為是生育的象徵，用來傳達祝願多子多孫、子孫萬代之意。南瓜的「南」與「男」同音，寓意男孩，生男孩是被古人普遍渴望和慶賀的，甚至延續至今。所以在婚禮上用紅色的瓜子招待客人，以祝願新人多子多孫。

pomegranate / This fruit stands for fertility because its many seeds, $zǐ$, are a play on the word for 'children,' $zǐ$. The image of a pomegranate halved to reveal its seeds signifies 'one hundred seeds, one hundred children' and is a common wedding gift. The pomegranate, the peach, and the Buddha's hand are three of the most auspicious fruits in China. When combined they constitute a wish for 'an abundance of children, longevity, and luck,' known as the 'three abundances,' $sān\ duō$.

石榴 ■ 古人稱石榴「千房同膜，千子如一」，從而用來隱喻生育。一幅畫著石榴半開的圖案，寓意「榴開百子」，是常用的結婚禮品。石榴、桃子和佛手組成中國三種最具吉祥意義的果品，寓意「三多」—多子、多壽、多福。

紅蛋 ■ 在婚禮中，新娘通常要按傳統做法，分派紅蛋給每一位前來賀喜的客人，以分享福氣和幸運。這個起源於江南的風俗已有相當長的歷史。今天，則以分送喜糖來替代，喜糖用紅紙包裝，上面印有雙喜字樣，也分派紅蛋給客人、家人和朋友，以慶賀嬰兒的新生、健康和好運。

red eggs / During wedding ceremonies, boiled eggs dyed red, *hóng dàn*, were traditionally distributed by the bride to everyone in attendance to share prosperity and good fortune. The custom began in Jiangnan Province and has a long history. Today the red eggs have been replaced with 'happiness candy,' *xǐ táng*, given out to the wedding guests. These candies are packaged in red shiny wrapping printed with the double happiness character. Boiled red eggs are also given to guests, family, and friends to celebrate a baby's health and continued good fortune.

紅蛋的傳說

三國時代的西蜀和東吳兩國只有聯合起來，才能對抗強大的北魏。但是，西蜀占了東吳的荊州不還，所以蜀、吳之間也矛盾重重。東吳都督周瑜想了個計謀，說動西蜀的劉備前來迎娶東吳公主孫尚香為妻，想用假招親、真扣留的策略，拿住劉備當人質，討還荊州。不料，這一計謀早被劉備的軍師諸葛亮識破。諸葛亮設下的「錦囊妙計」之一，即是「紅喜蛋計」。劉備上路時，帶上了大量染紅的雞蛋，一到東吳，馬上不論朝野上下，大小官將，逢人便送，一無遺漏。並說這是皇室禮儀，十分隆重。一般來客讓手下分，頭面人物還親自動手分，大造了「劉備招親」的輿論。東吳本來沒有這種風俗習慣，人人都感到新鮮和榮耀，便一傳十，十傳百，弄得家家戶戶都知道東吳公主孫尚香要與皇叔劉備成親了。結果，假戲真做，劉備得了個好夫人，歡天喜地，周瑜則「賠了夫人又折兵」。從此，江南添了個婚俗習慣，每逢結婚便分紅蛋，人人都可以討紅喜蛋，象徵新婚人家「龍鳳呈祥」。

legend of red eggs / During the Three Kingdoms period (220–265), the Wu and Shu empires were allies against the powerful Wei empire. However, the Shu empire claimed an area of land called Jingzhou belonging to the Wu empire. General Zhou Yu from Wu came up with a scheme to reclaim Jingzhou by inviting Shu's king, Liu Bei, to come to Wu on the false pretense that he would be given the hand of Princess Sun Shang Xiang in marriage. Liu Bei would be taken hostage in the Wu empire, and the general could then demand sovereignty over Jingzhou. But Liu Bei's astute military advisor, Zhu Ge Liang, immediately saw through his scheme and came up with a counterplan called the 'red happiness eggs strategy.' He played along with Zhou Yu's scheme, sending Liu Bei to the Wu empire with a great number of eggs dyed red with the message that they were gifts from the imperial palace in celebration of the wedding to come. Liu Bei distributed the red eggs to everyone he came across, and the news spread far and wide that he and the princess were to be married. With such widespread rejoicing in the air, Zhou Yu could not risk public outrage by taking Liu Bei hostage, and so the fake plan became a reality. Liu Bei was blessed with a wife, and the tradition of giving red eggs at weddings was born.

四喜娃 ■ 由兩個娃的頭、身、手、足巧妙連接，從上下左右四面可想象成四個娃娃，稱為「四喜娃」，意為四方童子並至，寓意子子孫孫綿延萬代。在明朝，四喜娃曾用青銅或黃銅鑄造。四喜娃的圖畫經常用作結婚禮品，或在嬰兒出生時，祝福其未來吉祥幸福。

four-happiness boys / A picture of two boys connected to create the illusion of four laughing boys is called the 'Four-Happiness Boys,' *sì xǐ wá.* Beginning in the Ming dynasty (1368–1644), their form was cast in bronze, brass, and copper. The image constitutes a wish for a happy marriage and generations of children and grandchildren. A picture of the four happiness boys is often given as a wedding gift or when a child is born, to wish the newlyweds or the baby a life filled with good fortune and happiness.

四喜娃的傳說

明初時，江西吉水出了個名叫解縉的神童，年方五歲，就把四書五經背得滾瓜爛熟。皇帝知道後，邀他去京城皇宮裡當面考核。解縉毫不費力地通過了考試，並經特許與秀才一起，進吉水縣學念書。

縣學教諭心想，這小家伙發跡太早，得殺殺他的傲氣。

一天，教諭命每個學生畫一幅瑞應圖。解縉畫一幅《如意靈芝》，教諭說太俗；再畫一幅《迎福納吉》，教諭說沒新意。解縉知他故意刁難，索性畫一幅雙頭八肢的連體娃娃交上去。

教諭看了暗喜：這下可以在全體學生面前，教訓教訓你了。他叱問解縉為何畫此怪胎，解縉回答說：「這是《四喜合局》呀。」教諭問是何四喜？解縉不慌不忙地答道：「久旱逢甘雨，他鄉遇故知，洞房花燭夜，金榜題名時。此為人生四喜。」教諭啞然失聲，以後再也不找解縉的茬兒了。

從此，連體娃娃就成為受人歡迎的吉祥圖。

legend of the four-happiness boys / During the Ming dynasty (1368–1644), a child prodigy by the name of Jie Jin lived in Jishui County, Jiangnan Province. By the age of five, the child had mastered the 'Four Books,' *Sì shū*, and the 'Five Classics,' *Wŭ jīng*, which make up the canon of the Confucian school of thought and are studied by scholars. When the emperor heard of this, he invited Jie Jin to the capital to sit for the imperial exams. He passed the exams without difficulty, then returned home to enter a school where he could study with the county's top scholars.

A teacher at the school thought the boy too young to have risen to such a position and wanted to humble him. One day he asked the students to draw a picture on the theme of the county's bumper harvest—a cause for great happiness. Jie Jin drew a picture of auspicious objects, and titled it '*rú yì* scepter with fungus of immortality,' *rú yì líng zhī.* The teacher found fault with his effort. The boy then drew another picture—'beckoning and acquiring good fortune,' *yíng fú nà jí*— but the teacher commented that it lacked originality.

Sensing that the teacher was deliberately making things difficult, Jie Jin then drew a figure with two heads and eight limbs. The teacher now reprimanded Jie Jin in front of all the students for drawing what appeared to be a deformed creature. Jie Jin responded that the picture was of 'four happinesses joined together,' *sì xĭ hé jú,* an image of four boys connected at the waist. The four happinesses, he explained, were the wedding night, passing the imperial exams, running into a friend in a faraway place, and rain after drought—all considered to be among life's major fortunes in ancient China. The teacher was dumbfounded and did not bother Jie Jin after that.

wealth

Wealth, *cái,* refers to prosperity attained through flourishing business, trade, or good harvests. It differs from the second level of happiness called 'prosperity,' *lù,* which refers to advancement in rank, position, or status. The desire for wealth and success does not have negative connotations but is viewed as a component of happiness. The Chinese surround themselves with images of wealth in the hope that their businesses will run smoothly, and that profit and fortune will soon come their way. Symbols that represent wealth include the goldfish, the number eight, gold and silver ingots, coins, the *fā cái* plant, and the God of Wealth.

財，指的是來自成功的生意、貿易或豐收所得的財富，與「五福」之二的「祿」略有不同，「祿」是決定於官階權位的俸給。在中國文化傳統裡，祈望高官厚祿，並不含有負面的意義，而是被視為福運來臨的好兆頭。中國人讓自己浸淫在生意興隆、大發利市、吉祥如意等追求財富的意念和形象之中。表達「財」的象徵，包括金魚、數字「八」、元寶、古錢、發菜以及財神。

「八」字 ■ 「八」，現在是最得人心的數字了，因為「八」與發財的「發」音近似，所以說「要得發，不離八」。電話號碼、車牌、房屋的街號等等都要用「八」字，有些地方甚至以荒唐的高價論售。有遠見的企業家開張營業，也要選擇帶有「八」的吉日。八月八日則被認為是農曆中非常吉利的日子。由於中國的方言繁多，有些地區「八」的發音不同，因此可能是不吉利的數字。

eight / The most auspicious number is the numeral eight, *bā*, because it rhymes with the word 'to prosper' or 'to attain wealth,' *fā*. There is a popular saying: 'if you want to be wealthy, don't be without the number eight,' *yào dé fā, bù lí bā*.

Telephone numbers, license plates, and house numbers with the number eight or, better yet, many eights, are much sought after and in some places can command exorbitant prices. When choosing a day to open a business, an entrepreneur looks for dates with the number eight. The eighth day of the eighth month is considered a very propitious date for the flourishing of wealth. Since the pronunciation of the word for eight differs in various dialects spoken in China, however, in some regions the number is not considered lucky.

「八」字 ■ 偶數一般被認為是吉數：「六」象徵「六六大順」，「二」表示「好事成雙」，但「四」卻是最不吉利的數字，因為「四」與「死」發音相似。一些最流行的數字組合為：三一八—生意發，一六八—一路發，二八二八—易發易發。

888 =

eight / Even numbers in general are considered lucky. The number six is symbolic for everything flowing smoothly. Two is also propitious as in the saying *háo shì chéng shuāng*, 'good things come in pairs.' However, the most inauspicious number is four, because it sounds identical to the Chinese word meaning 'to die,' *sǐ*.

Some of the most popular number combinations are:

318 = business will profit (*shēng yi fā*)
168 = on the road to wealth (*yī lù fā*)
2828 = easy to gain wealth (*yì fā yì fā*)

發發發 prosper, prosper, prosper (*fā fā fā*)

「八」字 ■ 明清時期，八寶紋被視為極為吉祥的符圖，每個樣式均繫以紅緞帶，而極為普遍地出現在服飾和陶瓷的裝飾上。道教有「暗八仙」：即漁鼓、寶劍、花籃、笊籬、葫蘆、扇子、陰陽板、橫笛。佛教有「八吉祥」：法輪、法螺、寶傘、白蓋、蓮花、寶瓶、金魚、盤長。也有用珠、錢、磬、祥雲、方勝、觥、書畫、紅葉、艾葉、蕉葉、鼎、靈芝、元寶、犀角等，從中選擇八種組成圖案稱八寶者。

eight / In the Ming and Qing dynasties (1368–1911), the eight Buddhist symbols, *bā jí xiáng,* and the eight treasures, *bā bǎo,* became popular motifs on garments and ceramics. The eight Buddhist symbols are the wheel, conch, umbrella, flag, lotus, vase, fish, and mystic knot. The eight treasures are eight charms each tied with a red ribbon, selected from a larger group of objects including the pearl, coin, stone chime, cloud, double lozenge (a headdress ornament symbolizing victory), wine vessel, book or drawing, leaf, fungus of immortality, gold and silver ingots, and rhinoceros horn. Another important group of symbols are the treasures of the Taoist Eight Immortals, called *àn bā xiān.*

god of wealth / The God of Wealth is worshiped far and wide, and his image is found in many homes and businesses. His portrait is easily identifiable by his long beard, official's gown, and distinct hat with ear flaps. It is tradition over Lunar New Year to invite the God of Wealth and offer manifold sacrifices at his shrine. Long ago, poor children went from house to house selling the God of Wealth's portrait. People could not refuse, as this would be rejecting affluence and a happy life.

There are two variations of Gods of Wealth—one from a civil background and one from a military background. Some stories describe the god as Bi Gan, a civil minister, or Fan Li, a civil leader, others as Zhao

財神 ■ 世人對財神的祭拜既深且廣，無論在商店或家庭裡，他的形象到處可見。那帶有帽翅的烏紗帽、長鬍子和官袍，使財神的畫像和神龕一下子就可以辨認出來。接財神和敬供豐富的祭品，是農曆新年期間一項重要傳統。很久以前，貧窮的孩子挨家挨戶地售賣財神像，人們很難拒絕他們，就是因為很難去拒絕對富裕和幸福生活的憧憬。

財神一般分文財神和武財神，文臣比干、范蠡和武將趙公明即是其中最流行的故事。源於道教傳說的趙公明，是被祭拜最廣的武財神。傳說他是陝西終南山人氏，秦朝時，避世山中，修道成仙。到元末明初，趙公明則被奉為財神。趙公明的典型形象為頭戴鐵冠，手執鐵鞭，面黑多鬚，跨一黑虎。道教信奉他能「驅雷役電，喚風喚雨，除瘟翦虐，保病禳災。」

Gong Ming, a military man. Zhao Gong Ming, of Taoist legend, is the most widely worshiped God of Wealth. He was not an actual historical figure, although he was said to be a general from Mount Zhongnan who fled to the mountains to cultivate a life of Taoism in the Qin dynasty (221–206 B.C.). It was not until the Ming dynasty (1368–1644) that he was deified as the God of Wealth. The most frequent representation of Zhao Gong Ming shows him with a black face and beard, wearing an iron helmet and holding an iron staff in one hand. He is believed to protect people from plague and to have control over lightning and thunder, wind and rain.

財神的傳說

趙公明原住峨嵋山，虔誠修煉，得道成仙，後應商代末代暴君紂王之請，下山迎戰周武王的軍師姜子牙。雙方都有威力無邊的法寶，剛一交戰，便各行道術。姜子牙的人馬成功地破了趙公明的絕招，奪走了他的兩樣法寶，逼迫他逃回商軍營中，不再出戰。接著，足智多謀的姜子牙扎了個稻草人，上書「趙公明」三字，親自焚符念咒，做法二十天。然後取桑弓桃箭，射穿稻草人的心坎和兩目，使趙公明恍忽沉迷，最後氣絕而死。商朝被推翻之後，姜子牙祭封神壇，敕封陣亡忠魂。由於他覺得殺趙公明是出於無奈，為此封德高望重的趙公明為財神，掌管迎祥納福，均衡分配和公平交易。

legend of the god of wealth / Zhao Gong Ming lived on the Taoist mountain of Emeishan and practiced asceticism. Known to perform astounding feats with his magical treasures, he answered the call of the tyrannical and last ruler of the Shang dynasty (1600–1027 B.C.) to aid in the battle against Jiang Zi Ya, a general under King Wu, of the state of Zhou. During battle, Jiang Zi Ya's men succeeded in seizing two of Zhao Gong Ming's treasures, forcing him to retreat to safe ground. Jiang Zi Ya then wrote his opponent's name on a straw doll and performed a ritual for twenty days. With a peachwood arrow he impaled the doll's eyes and heart, causing Zhao Gong Ming to become weak and die. After the Shang dynasty's defeat, Jiang Zi Ya honored the dead with venerable titles. As he felt he had had no choice but to kill Zhao Gong Ming, a moral and honorable man, he deified him as the God of Wealth. His duties were to uphold justice and ensure that wealth was evenly distributed.

legends of the god of wealth / Bi Gan, the uncle of Zhou, the last ruler of the Shang dynasty (1600–1027 B.C.), was a man of great virtue. Witnessing the ruler's tyrannical behavior, Bi Gan reproached him strongly. King Zhou was angered by this audacity and ordered Bi Gan's heart to be ripped from his body. King Zhou had heard that a wise man's heart had seven orifices and wished to see if this was true. Bi Gan removed his own heart and survived because he had consumed a potent elixir. Disillusioned, he left the palace to distribute his wealth to the common people. Due to the purity and honesty of his heart and deeds, he became known as the God of Wealth.

Another civil God of Wealth was Fan Li, who lived during the Spring Autumn period (770–480 B.C.). China was divided into many small countries, including Qi Country and Yue Country, where Fan Li was from. He was a wealthy businessman who had been an influential official under King Gao Jian. He counseled the king on important matters and aided him in conquering King Fu Cha of Wu Country. When the king rewarded his officials, Fan Li departed for Qi Country, preferring a life of anonymity. There he involved himself in agriculture and business and went on to become very wealthy. Since he had previously occupied a high position and possessed great wealth, he was not concerned with money. He became wealthy three times in his life and each time gave his money to the poor or to his friends and relatives. As a result of his generosity and good fortune, people honored him as the God of Wealth.

財神的傳說

比干是商代紂王的叔父，為人忠耿正直。比干見紂王荒淫失政，暴虐無道，常常直言強諫，但紂王卻惱怒無比，竟命比干剖膛挖心。因為他要看看，聖人的心有七孔的傳聞是否真的。比干自剖其腹，摘心擲地，走出宮門。由於他服了姜子牙的丹藥，故不得死，來到民間，廣散財寶。鑒於他心地正直純潔，行為無偏無私，所以被擁戴為文財神。

另一位文財神是春秋時代越國的范蠡，他倒是個經商發財的大富商。范蠡本是越王勾踐手下得力的大臣，他給越王出謀劃策，幫助越王打敗吳國，成就了霸業。當越王大賞功臣時，范蠡逃出是非之地，離開越國，到了齊國。他在齊國隱姓埋名，經營農業和商業，發了大財。由於范蠡曾經歷過高官厚祿，所以不在乎錢財，他三次發財，三次都把所得錢財分散給窮人或親戚朋友。范蠡能發家致富又能散財，所以人們就尊崇他為文財神。

Fan Li, civil God of Wealth.

文財神范蠡

古錢　■　銅製古錢產生於戰國晚期。其形狀外圓法天，內方法地，上面經常鑄有吉祥文字，如「長命富貴」、「吉祥如意」等，從前成為財富與富貴的象徵。

商店門前掛兩枚古錢，代表財神，以招財進寶，用紅繩進結兩枚古錢，結成一個護符，寓意「連錢」。這對做生意是特別吉利的意象。用紅線將古錢串成的項鍊，能為佩戴者避邪納福。古錢也是「八寶」之一，象徵具有神力，為人們帶來好運。「八寶」圖案經常應用於陶瓷、刺繡和綢帶上。

由於「錢」與「前」同聲同韻，古錢上的孔又稱「眼」，組合成「眼前」之意，所以與其它許多事物例如與喜鵲相配在一起，就構成「喜在眼前」的寓意。

coins / Copper coins originated in the late Warring States period (480–221 B.C.). Round on the outside with a square hole in the center, these ancient coins became a potent symbol of wealth and prosperity. The circular shape represents heaven, and the internal square signifies earth.

Often the coins are inscribed with lucky phrases such as *cháng mìng fù guì*, 'a long life of wealth and abundance,' or *jí xiáng rú yì*, 'as much luck as you wish.'

A picture of two coins hung above a shop door represents the God of Wealth and attracts wealth to a business. Coins strung together with red thread form a charm to bring a 'continuous flow of wealth,' *lián qián*, which is especially auspicious for business. Necklaces made from red thread and coins offer protection from evil spirits and bring luck to the wearer. The coin is also one of the eight treasures, *bā bǎo*, symbols that possess the power to draw good fortune.

Used as a play on words, 'coin' can mean 'before one's eyes,' because the hole in the center is known as an 'eye,' *yǎn*, and the coin itself, *qián*, is a rebus for 'before.' Any number of objects can be paired with the coin in this context. For example, the 'magpie,' *xǐ que*, is a symbol of conjugal happiness, and thus its image in conjunction with a coin conveys the message 'happiness before your eyes,' *xǐ zài yǎn qián*.

money tree / A picture of a tree laden with strings of coins is a wish for affluence. Under the tree, the God of Wealth and others enjoy the ripe abundance of money. This scene is called *yáo qián shù*, and literally means 'shaking money tree.'

搖錢樹 ■ 掛滿一串串古錢的搖錢樹，象徵著對富貴的祝願，圖中描繪樹下的財神以及人們從搖錢樹上豐收的喜悅。

橘　■　橘與「吉」音相似，人們以橘喻「吉」，表祝吉之意，橘遂成為新春佳節中最受歡迎的吉祥物。同樣，「雞」與「吉」發音相似，所以雞也是新年期間流行的佳肴。「大吉大利」則是新年期間最流行的吉祥語。

tangerine / One of the most popular fruits during the New Year celebration is the tangerine, because *jú*, 'tangerine,' is close to *jí*, 'auspicious' or 'lucky.' *Jú* also sounds similar to *zhù fú*, a wish for good fortune. The popular phrase *dà jí dà lì* expresses the sentiment 'may you enjoy an abundance of fortune and profits.'

橘 ■ 在中國南方，每逢新春佳節，許多家庭和商店都會買一盆金橘，象掛滿金錢的「搖錢樹」一樣，或作為禮物，或作為擺飾，預兆新年發財，四季吉運。

畫幾個大橘，表示「大吉」。柿子和橘子組成的圖畫，「柿」與「事」諧音，寓意「事事大吉」。

tangerine / In southern China, many households and businesses buy a small budding tangerine plant to bring wealth and peace. These are called 'golden tangerines,' *jīn jú*, and the fruit looks like gold coins hanging on a tree. The plants are often exchanged as gifts and should never be refused, because the recipient would be turning away 'wealth and luck in all things.' Two large tangerines, *dà jú*, represent an 'abundance of auspiciousness,' *dà jí*. A picture of a tangerine and a persimmon means 'an abundance of luck in everything one does,' *shì shì dà jí*: the word for persimmon sounds the same as 'everything,' *shì*, and the tangerine stands for luck.

金銀元寶 ■ 元寶，是鞋狀的金銀錠塊，在封建時代作為貨幣使用。元寶形的金錠在漢代就已出現，直到元代才定型為銀元寶。元寶的「元」與「源」同音，代表「財源」之意。在年畫中，元寶通常都是象徵富貴的吉祥物。在新年裡招待客人的「元寶茶」，就是取元寶之吉祥含意而命名的。

gold and silver ingots /
The *yuán bǎo* is a shoe-shaped ingot used as money in feudal China. Its name literally means 'original treasure.' The *yuán bǎo* first appeared in the Han dynasty (206 B.C.–A.D. 220) made of gold, although it was not until the Yuan dynasty (1279–1368) that they became a standardized currency and were made of silver. The first character of *yuán bǎo* has the same sound as the word for 'source,' *yuán*, and 'financial resources,' *cái yuán*, so ingots are regularly featured as an auspicious symbol for wealth in New Year pictures. A lucky tea, *yuán bǎo chá*, served during New Year, is also named after the ingots.

dumpling / *Jiǎo zi* resemble the shape of ancient Chinese money, or ingots, *yuán bǎo*, and therefore symbolize the wish for wealth. These dumplings are named after a currency, *jiǎo zi*, which is a play on a term for the junction of the old year and the new. Consequently, in northern China meat-filled dumplings are eaten at midnight on New Year's Eve to promote good fortune and wealth in the year ahead. In Shanghai, Hangzhou, and Suzhou, egg dumplings are golden colored to look like gold ingots.

The tradition of inserting a coin into one or more dumplings began in the Song dynasty (960–1279). Anyone fortunate enough to pick a lucky dumpling would enjoy endless wealth and prosperity for the upcoming year. This custom is still practiced in northern China on New Year's Eve.

餃子 ■ 「交子」是指新舊年相交的時辰「子時」，「交」與「餃」諧音，「餃子」的命名即由此而來。在中國北方，新年除夕子夜時刻吃肉餡的「更歲餃子」，則意味著廣拓財運。而餃子的形狀酷似中國古代的錢幣元寶，所以也成為富貴的象徵。上海、杭州、蘇州有顏色金黃燦爛的「蛋角」，看上去就象金元寶。

將一枚或數枚銅錢包入餃子的風俗源於宋朝，吃著這枚餃子的幸運者，會被認為在新的一年中財源不斷。這個風俗至今仍在北方過新年時流行。

red packet / During the New Year celebrations, elders give children 'lucky money,' *yā suì qián*. The custom arose from the belief that children were easily susceptible to harm and that the money, *qián*, would protect them from evil spirits. This lucky money also served to bring good fortune for the upcoming year. The term *yā suì qián* literally means 'to press down evil,' because *yā* means 'to press' and *suì* is the name of an evil spirit that comes out on New Year's Eve to harm children. Another traditional practice was to thread coins together with red string—red being a lucky color—and place them underneath a child's bed. Coins tied together were sometimes formed into the shapes of auspicious creatures and objects, such as the carp, the

紅包 ■ 新年期間，老年人經常給孩子們派「壓歲錢」，這個風俗源起於人們相信孩子最易受傷害，「歲」即是「年」，而「年」傳說為新春期間出山吃人的獨角獸，給「壓歲錢」就是要用錢壓住它，保佑孩子來年得好運。另一做法則是，將古錢用吉祥的紅色絲線串起來，放在孩子的床底下，以避災祛邪。古錢串起來經常還被扎製成鯉魚、龍或如意金鉤等物狀。

今天，農曆新年期間，銅錢和吉祥文字已改為封入紅包，所有的孩子以及未婚年輕人，都可以從老一輩人及已婚朋友那裡得到紅包。紅包祝福孩子們新年健康、努力學習。

dragon, or the *rú yì* scepter.
Today, during New Year, coins
or notes are placed in red
envelopes, *hóng bāo*. All children and young people who
have not yet married are eligible
to receive these red packets
from elders or married friends.
The red packets wish them
good health on New Year and
encourage them to study hard.

legend of the red packet / There was once an evil spirit by the name of Sui who emerged each year on New Year's Eve to harm people. When children were sleeping soundly in their beds, this demon with a black body and white hands would enter their homes and reach out to touch its victim's head three times. The frightened child would let out a scream, break out in a fever, and begin to mumble deliriously. Once the fever had subsided, the family would discover that their smart child had turned into a simpleton.

One New Year's Eve, a child was playing with a piece of red paper and eight copper coins. The youngster wrapped and unwrapped them until he grew drowsy and fell asleep with the package beside his pillow. Suddenly, during the night, a strong gust of wind blew open the door and extinguished the light. The white hand of Sui reached out for the child's head, but all at once, a flash of light shot out from the red package beside the pillow. Sui was terrified and quickly raced away. The custom of staying up all night on New Year's Eve and giving children red packets to protect themselves from Sui became known as *shǒu suì*, 'to protect from Sui.'

紅包的傳說

「歲」是每到新年除夕就出山危害百姓的惡鬼，當小孩子在床上酣睡時，白手黑身的「歲」會潛入房間，觸摸他們的頭部三次。小孩因此受驚嚇而發出尖叫，會突然發高燒，並昏迷說糊話。高燒退了之後，家人將發現聰明的孩子已變成了白痴。

某一年的除夕，一個小孩正在用一張紅紙和八枚銅錢包著玩，包了拆，拆了又包，直玩到累了而昏昏入睡，紅紙包則留在枕頭旁。突然，一陣狂風刮起，吹開房門，撲滅燭光。「歲」乘著夜色，潛入房間，在用白手去觸摸小孩頭部的同時，一道閃光從枕頭旁的紅包射出，「歲」驚恐逃竄。從此，除夕守夜不睡，分派紅包給孩子們，以保護他們避開「歲」的危害，就形成了「守歲」的風俗。

神仙劉海 ■ 劉海是道教傳說中的人物，原為五代時期燕王的丞相，後來成為財神的替身。劉海經常被描繪成手執串有金錢的彩線，在逗弄一隻三足金蟾。這隻金蟾被認為是靈物，能使劉海想去那兒就去那兒。金蟾潛入井底逃去，劉海就用彩繩串起金錢，將它引出。《劉海戲金蟾》是一個家喻戶曉的故事。

god liu hai / A figure from Taoist legend, Liu Hai was a government minister who lived in the Five Dynasties period (907–960). Now a symbol of wealth, he is often depicted holding a string of ancient Chinese coins and accompanied by a lucky three-legged toad. The creature possessed supernatural qualities and could take Liu Hai wherever he wished to go. However, the toad was known to disappear down wells, and Liu Hai would lure him out with gold coins threaded on string. The story 'Liu Hai plays with Gold and Toad,' *Liú Hǎi xì jīn chán*, is a well-known folktale.

劉海的傳說

一天，一個自稱阿保的男子，上門求見蘇州大富商貝宏文，請求做他的僕人，貝宏文答應了。阿保幹活很賣力，還顯出獨特的性情，有時幾天不吃也不餓，給他工錢，堅辭不受。一次，他從井裡汲水時，竟拉出一隻三足大蟾蜍，並「以彩繩數尺繫之」，歡躍地逗著戲耍。阿保告訴主人說：「此物逃去，期年不能得，今尋得之矣。」於是鄉裡傳述，爭往看之。此時，蜂湧而至的村民只見劉海「負蟾者舉手謝主人，從庭中冉冉乘空而去。」人們這才認出，阿保就是為尋蟾蜍而投傭的神仙劉海。

legend of god liu hai / One day a boy named A Bao came to the door of a wealthy merchant by the name of Bei Hong Wen, who lived in Suzhou. He begged the man to take him in as his servant. The man agreed, and A Bao worked extremely hard. When it was time for Bei Hong Wen to pay him, A Bao refused to accept his salary. Among A Bao's other peculiar traits, he would sometimes go without eating for days. One day A Bao was fetching water from the well when he pulled up a three-legged toad. Overjoyed, he played with the toad, amusing it with a multicolored piece of string. He told Bei Hong Wen that he had finally found his toad, which had run away over a year ago. News spread, and the people from the village came to see the toad. As they gathered around, they witnessed A Bao, with the toad on his shoulder, say farewell to Bei Hong Wen and slowly ascend to the sky. The people realized that A Bao was the immortal god Liu Hai, who had come in the guise of a servant in search of his toad.

fish / Since the word for 'fish' and the word for 'plenty,' *yú*, are pronounced the same, fish have come to represent abundance. Fish are very auspicious during New Year, and the saying 'may there be abundance year after year,' *nián nián yǒu yú*, is often written alongside a picture of fish in a basket. A whole fish is a popular dish served for New Year's Eve dinner. It is a good omen to leave the bones along with the head and tail intact to symbolize surplus and also a good beginning and end.

An image of a child holding an oversized fish and a lotus flower is a common New Year picture that means 'successive years of abundance,' *lián nián yǒu yú*. This is because one word for 'lotus flower,' *lián*, is pronounced the same as the word for 'continuous.'

魚 ■ 魚在新年期間是非常吉祥的象徵，「魚」諧音「餘」，寓意「年年有餘」。這句吉祥語常與畫一籃魚的圖案貼在一起。正是這個原因，在新年除夕吃「年夜飯」時，「全魚」就不可少。人在吃「全魚」時，魚頭與魚尾要完好保留，以討個好口彩，不僅象徵「有餘」，而且「有頭有尾」。畫一個兒童抱著一條特大鯉魚，並與蓮花在一起的年畫，寓意「連年有魚」，因「蓮」與「連」同音。

goldfish / The characters for goldfish, *jīn yú*, sound identical to those meaning 'abundance of gold,' making the goldfish a frequent symbol of wealth and abundance. One of the most popular New Year's images is a child holding a large goldfish and a lotus flower, *hé*, which brings both wealth and harmony, *hé*. A goldfish wrapped in a lotus leaf is commonly found on New Year's cards and means 'an abundance of gold in your wallet,' as *hé bāo* also means 'wallet.' A bowl full of goldfish, *jīn yú mǎn táng*, means 'may gold and jade fill your house,' because the pronunciation of 'fish,' *yú*, is the same except for tone to 'jade,' *yù*.

金魚 ■ 金魚與「金餘」諧音，從而成為富足的象徵。一幅最為流行的年畫描繪一個兒童，抱著一條大金魚，配以荷花，「荷」即「和」，表達富足與和諧之祝願。賀年卡中也可以看到用大荷葉包裹著一條金魚的圖畫，「荷包」即錢包，表示「金滿錢包」之意。一滿缸金魚，「金魚」與「金玉」諧音，寓意「金玉滿堂」。

金魚 goldfish (*jīn yú*) =

金餘 abundance of gold (*jīn yú*)

發菜 ■ 細髮似的發菜只在中國西北的戈壁灘上生長，由於稀少，導至其價甚高。「發菜」與「發財」音近，也就成了發財的同義詞，人們為了圖吉利，總要在新年晚宴上吃這道菜。在中國南方，發菜常與粉絲、蠔豉相配為菜，「蠔豉」與「好事」音近，取其吉祥口彩。

fā cái plant = to become wealthly (*fā cái*)

fā cái plant / A dried, stringy black plant that resembles hair, *fā cái* grows in the Gobi Desert of northwest China, and is highly priced due to its scarcity. The plant is a symbol of wealth because the name sounds like the term 'to become wealthy,' *fā cái*, so the plant is commonly served at New Year's dinners. In southern China, it is prepared with thin rice noodles, *fěn sī*, and dried oysters, *háo*, adding still more luck, as *háo* sounds like the first character in 'good events,' *háo shì*.

lettuce / *Shēng cài*, 'lettuce,' contains the word *cái*, meaning 'wealth,' and eating it expresses the wish for an abundance of wealth. The first character, *shēng*, also means 'birth,' and therefore lettuce is often eaten during New Year's festival to signify the birth of a new year.

During the New Year lion dance, lettuce or other green vegetables, *cài*, are offered to the lion. When the lion performs a dance and eats the offering, it is an omen of wealth and prosperity.

生菜 ■ 生菜發音與「生財」相近，而被列為有吉祥意義的食品。生菜的「生」同時也含有「誕生」之意，所以，在農曆新年吃生菜，又寓意祝賀新年之誕生。在新年期間舞獅，生菜和其它蔬菜，被賦予「財」的含意，而成為獅舞的道具，舞獅吃生菜，即是發財致富的好兆頭。

招財貓 ■ 許多中國人的商店和企業，都將招財貓作為財運和成功的護符，放在入口處。招財貓一般用陶土製成，尺寸大小不同。正如其名稱所示，招財貓坐鎮門口，招呼客人入內花錢購物。招財貓源於日本，但已成為中國人祈求財運的重要標誌。

beckoning cat / The *zhāo cái māo*, or 'beckoning cat,' can be found at the entrances to many Chinese businesses. Commonly made of ceramic and found in a wide variety of sizes, it serves as a charm for wealth and success. The name means literally 'inviting wealth cat,' because the feline sits by the door and invites people in to spend their money. The beckoning cat originated in Japan but has become an important symbol of wealth to the Chinese.

index

a
A Bao, 241
apples, 49

b
Bai Ju Yi, 30
bamboo, 117–18, 119, 146, 189
bats, 19, 33–34
Bei Hong Wen, 241
Bi Gan, 220, 224
Buddha, 195
Buddha's hand, 19, 62–63, 200

c
Canopus (star), 107
Cao Guo Jiu, 140
carp, 71, 80, 185
cats, beckoning, 12, 249
Chang E, 132–33
chestnuts, 197
children, lucky, 46–47
chrysanthemums, 112, 144–45
clocks, 9
clouds, 59, 218
coins, 211, 218, 226–27, 228, 234–35
Confucius, 53, 66, 178
crabs, 90
cranes, 75, 97, 112, 123–24, 125, 130, 143
cypress, 120

d
Da A Fu, 46, 47
dates, 196, 197
death, 9, 83
deer, 71, 74–76, 143
Ding Ling Wei, 124
door gods, 36, 39–40, 44, 45, 127
double happiness, 119, 156–57

character, 156–57, 163, 165–66
God of, 167–68
dragon dance, 55
dragons, 53, 80, 178–79
ducks, mandarin, 157, 174, 177
dumplings, 233
Dusu Mountain, 40, 89

e
eggs, red, 201, 203
eight immortals, 138, 140, 218
eight (number), 12, 211, 214, 217–18
examinations, imperial, 70, 80, 90

f
fā cái plant, 211, 246–47
Fan Li, 220, 224–25
fertility, 156, 157, 198–200
firecrackers, 118, 189–90
fish, 218, 242
fortune cookies, 66
four-happiness boys, 205, 207
four (number), 217
Fu Cha, 224
fungus of immortality, 59, 75, 97, 109, 142–43, 218

g
Gao Jian, 224
ginseng, 147
goldfish, 211, 244
Gong Qin, 27
gourds, 50–51
Guan Yin, 140

h
Han Shan, 191, 193
Han Xiang Zi, 140
He Xian Gu, 140
Hong Fu, 177

horses, 86
Hou Yi, 132–33

i
ingots, 88, 211, 218, 232, 233

j
Jiang Zi Ya, 223
Jie Jin, 207

k
Kunlun Mountains, 109, 130

l
Lan Cai He, 140
Lantern Festival, 55
laughing mouth, 65
lettuce, 248
lion dance, 55, 248
Li Tie Guai, 50, 140
Liu Bei, 203
Liu Hai, 238, 241
lock, longevity, 150–51
Long Du, 140
longevity, 94–95, 97
    character, 100–102, 105
    Goddess of, 134–35, 137
    God of, 12, 13, 14, 75, 77, 97, 107–10, 135
    symbols of, 97
lotus, 157, 194–95, 218, 242, 244
luck, 18–19
    character, 18–19, 23, 27
    God of, 12, 13, 14, 19, 29, 30, 77, 107
    symbols of, 19
Lu Dong Bin, 140

m
magpies, 157, 171, 173, 227
Ma Gu, 134–35, 137
Ma Qiu, 137

marriage, 156–57, 163, 171, 174
melons, 199
Meng Chang, 44
Mo Jie, 140
money tree, 228
Monkey King, 51, 128
monkeys, 71, 86
Moon Goddess, 132–33

n
narcissus, 146
New Year pictures, 45, 49, 232
nine (number), 152
Nong Yu, 180
noodles, longevity, 94, 149
North Pole, star of, 110

o
one hundred (number), 120
oysters, 67

p
packets, red, 234–35
Pan Gu, 125
peace, 49
Peace and Harmony, Gods of, 56, 157
peaches, 63, 94, 97, 127–28, 130, 200
peachwood charms, 40, 44, 45, 127
peanuts, 198
peonies, 71, 85
persimmons, 120, 230
phoenix, 178–80
pine trees, 97, 112, 115, 117, 120, 123
pinwheels, 60
plums, 117, 119
pomegranates, 63, 157, 200

prosperity, 70–71, 210
God of, 12, 13, 14, 71, 77–78, 107
symbols of, 71
pumpkin seeds, 198–99
puns, 11
Pure Spirit Mountain, 124

q
qí lín, 182
Qin Qiong (Qin Shu Bao), 39
Qin Shi Huangdi, 108, 182
Queen Mother of the West, 97, 128, 130, 132, 134–35, 140

r
rebuses, 11, 12
red (color), 43, 157, 163, 189
rice cakes, sticky, 91
roosters, 89
Ru Lai, 140

s
scepter, 19, 29, 56, 59, 143
Shen Tu, 40, 89
Shi De, 191, 193
shrimp, 64
six (number), 83, 217
South Pole, star of, 110
spiders, 186
spring couplets, 43–44

t
Tai Zong, 39
Tai Zu, 44
tangerines, 229–30
tortoises, 123, 125
two (number), 217

u
Unity and Harmony, Gods of, 191, 193

v
vases, 49, 56, 85, 218

w
Wang An Shi, 165–66
Wang Fang Ping, 137
Wang Xiang, 112
Wang Yuan Bao, 248
Wan Hui, 193
wealth, 71, 210–11
God of, 211, 220–21, 223–25, 227, 228
symbols of, 211
White Snake, 109
windmills, 60
Wu Di, 30, 128

x
Xiao Shi, 180
Xuan Zong, 149
Xu Xian, 109

y
Yan Chao, 110
Yang Cheng, 30
Yang Mei, 177
Ye Wang Zi, 40
Yuan Ge, 177
Yu Chi Gong (Yu Chi Jingde), 39
Yu Lei, 40, 89

z
Zhang Dao Ling, 30
Zhang Guo Lao, 140
Zhao Gong Ming, 220–21, 223
Zhao Qu, 115
Zhong Li Quan, 140
Zhou, 224
Zhou Yu, 203
Zhu Ge Liang, 203
Zhu Yuan Zhang, 27

acknowledgments

Thanks to Patrick Wu, who enthusiastically spent many hours of his spare time researching and sending material for this book. To Vanessa Holle, who helped put together the very first mock-up of this book, and offered trusted advice along the way. To Norman Bock for supporting the project and offering a network of contacts. To Sing Lin for helping me with many unusual requests throughout the project. To Sarah Shang for spending valuable time aiding in translating difficult Chinese passages and answering questions. To wordsmith Jeremy Mende, who offered his critique and time on the manuscript. To Judith Dunham and Elizabeth Bell for their copyediting expertise. Thanks to You Shan Tang for sharing his wealth of knowledge of traditional Chinese culture, to Uncle William H. Ying for looking over the Chinese text, and to Jennifer West for last-hour feedback. At Chronicle Books, many thanks go to Jan Hughes, Steve Kim, and Shona Bayley for taking the greatest care in the production of the book.

In China, many thanks go to friends: Wei Wang Qing, who helped research at Beijing Library; Wei Pei Pin, who aided in finding material in bookstores; and to Wan Le, who helped interview people on my travels. To friends, Sun Shan, Zhu Nan, Shao Jun Yang, and Chen Hai Ping, who answered numerous questions, and to Sun Ji Pei and Uncle Sun Ji Gang, who accompanied me on my travels throughout China and supported my endeavors along the way.

Lastly, thanks to my wonderful editor, Jay Schaefer, for his friendship, patience, and sense of humor; and to Pamela Geismar, design director at Chronicle Books, for her support and understanding throughout the project.

biographies

betsy wang

vivien sung / was born and raised in Sydney, Australia, where she began working as a graphic designer before moving to New York and San Francisco, where she now lives. She has studied in Beijing and travels frequently to China. This is the first book she has written. Her Web site is www.fivefoldhappiness.com

you shan tang / graduated from Beijing University, where he studied Chinese literature and painting, and received a masters at the Central Academy of Fine Arts, Beijing. He lives in San Francisco.

作者簡介

孫維文 ■ 生長在澳洲悉尼，曾任平面設計師，後來移居紐約，現定居三藩市。她曾在北京學習中文，並經常去中國旅遊。這是她寫的第一本書。她的網址是：www.fivefoldhappiness.com

唐又山 ■ 畢業於北京大學中文系和北京中央美術學院美術史系，現定居三藩市，從事繪畫與寫作。

五福